THE CENTRAL AFRICAN REPUBLIC: FROM "PRE-GENOCIDE" TO GENOCIDE?

HEARING

BEFORE THE

SUBCOMMITTEE ON AFRICA, GLOBAL HEALTH, GLOBAL HUMAN RIGHTS, AND INTERNATIONAL ORGANIZATIONS

OF THE

COMMITTEE ON FOREIGN AFFAIRS HOUSE OF REPRESENTATIVES

ONE HUNDRED THIRTEENTH CONGRESS

SECOND SESSION

MAY 1, 2014

Serial No. 113–180

Printed for the use of the Committee on Foreign Affairs

Available via the World Wide Web: http://www.foreignaffairs.house.gov/ or
http://www.gpo.gov/fdsys/

U.S. GOVERNMENT PRINTING OFFICE

87–715PDF   WASHINGTON : 2014

For sale by the Superintendent of Documents, U.S. Government Printing Office
Internet: bookstore.gpo.gov   Phone: toll free (866) 512–1800; DC area (202) 512–1800
Fax: (202) 512–2104   Mail: Stop IDCC, Washington, DC 20402–0001

COMMITTEE ON FOREIGN AFFAIRS

EDWARD R. ROYCE, California, *Chairman*

CHRISTOPHER H. SMITH, New Jersey
ILEANA ROS-LEHTINEN, Florida
DANA ROHRABACHER, California
STEVE CHABOT, Ohio
JOE WILSON, South Carolina
MICHAEL T. McCAUL, Texas
TED POE, Texas
MATT SALMON, Arizona
TOM MARINO, Pennsylvania
JEFF DUNCAN, South Carolina
ADAM KINZINGER, Illinois
MO BROOKS, Alabama
TOM COTTON, Arkansas
PAUL COOK, California
GEORGE HOLDING, North Carolina
RANDY K. WEBER SR., Texas
SCOTT PERRY, Pennsylvania
STEVE STOCKMAN, Texas
RON DeSANTIS, Florida
DOUG COLLINS, Georgia
MARK MEADOWS, North Carolina
TED S. YOHO, Florida
LUKE MESSER, Indiana

ELIOT L. ENGEL, New York
ENI F.H. FALEOMAVAEGA, American
   Samoa
BRAD SHERMAN, California
GREGORY W. MEEKS, New York
ALBIO SIRES, New Jersey
GERALD E. CONNOLLY, Virginia
THEODORE E. DEUTCH, Florida
BRIAN HIGGINS, New York
KAREN BASS, California
WILLIAM KEATING, Massachusetts
DAVID CICILLINE, Rhode Island
ALAN GRAYSON, Florida
JUAN VARGAS, California
BRADLEY S. SCHNEIDER, Illinois
JOSEPH P. KENNEDY III, Massachusetts
AMI BERA, California
ALAN S. LOWENTHAL, California
GRACE MENG, New York
LOIS FRANKEL, Florida
TULSI GABBARD, Hawaii
JOAQUIN CASTRO, Texas

AMY PORTER, *Chief of Staff*   THOMAS SHEEHY, *Staff Director*
JASON STEINBAUM, *Democratic Staff Director*

———

SUBCOMMITTEE ON AFRICA, GLOBAL HEALTH, GLOBAL HUMAN RIGHTS, AND INTERNATIONAL ORGANIZATIONS

CHRISTOPHER H. SMITH, New Jersey, *Chairman*

TOM MARINO, Pennsylvania
RANDY K. WEBER SR., Texas
STEVE STOCKMAN, Texas
MARK MEADOWS, North Carolina

KAREN BASS, California
DAVID CICILLINE, Rhode Island
AMI BERA, California

CONTENTS

THE CENTRAL AFRICAN REPUBLIC: FROM "PRE–GENOCIDE" TO GENOCIDE?

THURSDAY, MAY 1, 2014

House of Representatives,
Subcommittee on Africa, Global Health,
Global Human Rights, and International Organizations,
Committee on Foreign Affairs,
Washington, DC.

The subcommittee met, pursuant to notice, at 10 o'clock a.m., in room 2172 Rayburn House Office Building, Hon. Christopher H. Smith (chairman of the subcommittee) presiding.

Mr. Smith. The subcommittee will come to order and thank you for being here and good morning to everyone. Our hearing addresses an extremely critical topic this morning, the worsening crisis in the Central African Republic where untold lives hang in the balance and the window for action is narrowing each and every day.

This is not the first hearing that we have had on the Central African Republic. It follows up on a hearing that we held last November, and of course many of us, like our distinguished witnesses, have been in ongoing and numerous meetings with bishops, imams, humanitarian NGOs, diplomats, and interested parties.

I would note that at our November hearing, Acting Assistant Secretary Robert Jackson who will again testify today said that the CAR was in a pre-genocide stage. Since that time that Mr. Jackson spoke to us, the situation appears to have gotten demonstratively worse.

We will hear again today from Acting Assistant Secretary Jackson who will update us not only on the situation on the ground, but also on a changing policy that I believe reflects a course of action that we had recommended that the administration undertake last November—namely, that the United Nations peacekeepers be introduced into the country, as the existing African force has been serving far too many vested interests.

Hopefully such an intervention will not come too late, because we are witnessing a country that is in rapid disintegration, apparently descending again from a pre-genocide stage to one characterized by a word almost too painful to articulate, genocide.

For in a country that for decades has been characterized by brutal misrule and brazen corruption, we are seeing for the first time sectarian divisions that never existed before. Economic tensions and rivalry over land use for grazing versus planting have always existed, but they have given way to a butchery based on religious and ethnic affiliation.

This is happening at a time when we mark the 20th anniversary of the genocide in Rwanda. When that country was being turned into a massive killing field the world stood idly by. Both President Clinton and the U.N. peacekeeping chief at the time, Kofi Annan, had actionable intelligence information that could have prevented, or at least mitigated, the Rwandan genocide, but chose callous indifference that enabled slaughter of unprecedented proportions.

I would note parenthetically that I held a series of meetings—hearings, three of them—on Rwanda, and we heard from people who said we had the information in hand. General Dallaire was there on the ground willing to take effective action to curtail what turned out to be upwards of 1 million people who were slaughtered, and with that information again that could have been prevented or at least largely mitigated.

When the blood stopped flowing, the world looked at the corpses piled high and was shocked. ''Never again'' was the phrase that was on everyone's lips. Well, ladies and gentlemen, it is happening again as we know, as our distinguished witnesses know and will bear witness to today. The question before us today is whether the phrase ''never again'' is one that we simply use to pay lip service while nothing is being done or not enough, and whether or not we are going to act decisively.

We do have two distinguished witnesses from the State Department here today, and as I mentioned Acting Assistant Secretary Jackson and also Anne Richard, Assistant Secretary for Population, Refugees, and Migration.

While the State Department sending two people to testify is very encouraging, as it shows a heightened commitment to the issue, the question I will be asking them to answer is not what are we doing, but are we doing enough?

In 2012, the administration, to much fanfare, created an Atrocities Prevention Board following a Presidential Study Directive which stated that ''Preventing mass atrocities and genocide is a core national security interest and a core moral responsibility of the United States.''

The APB is supposed to provide early warning of mass atrocities and mobilized interagency resources to stop such atrocities. But where has the Board been? Did we take our eyes off the ball in the CAR, perhaps because we are confronted by so many other crises? While we have taken some steps including authorizing $170 million in humanitarian and peacekeeping aid, something we hope to hear more about from our Government witnesses, are such resources adequate given the magnitude of the problem?

We have a situation in a country where of the population of roughly 5.2 million people, 1.3 million are at risk of starvation while 2.5 million are estimated to be in need of other forms of humanitarian assistance—that is nearly half the country. We are seeing ethnic cleansing whereby whole villages are being emptied and a countryside laid waste.

There are more than 600,000 internally displaced persons in the CAR, plus more than 320,000 others who are refugees in neighboring countries. Illustrative of how the situation has worsened, the total number of those displaced has doubled since the time we held our hearing last November when it was estimated at 460,000 CAR nationals displaced.

Accurate figures for the numbers killed are hard to come by and we hope our witnesses will be able to shed some light on that. We are told that an estimated 2,000 people have been killed since December alone, but I believe that number is probably a conservative estimate.

What reports we do receive, however, are blood-curdling. Human Rights Watch reported on an attack of a Muslim neighborhood in the town of Guen in the early morning hours of February 1, by so-called anti-balaka forces. A father recounted how as the family was fleeing he saw his 10-year-old boy shot in the leg and fall down. The child was then set upon by men with machetes who hacked at him until he was dead.

Four days later, in what was reminiscent of the massacre in Srebrenica in former Yugoslavia, anti-Balaka forces came upon a group of Muslims who were in hiding. They separated the men from the women and small children and executed the men, 45 of them, using machetes and then shooting those who lay wounded.

Through the decades, the CAR has been beset by violence and misrule. Such religious-based violence though is something that is a new phenomenon. How did the country get to this point? What began as a political coup d'etat in March 2013 against former President Francois Bozize by Michel Djotodia quickly took on religious and ethnic overtones.

As we detailed in our November hearing, Djotodia came to power with the military backing of Seleka, a militia of some 25,000 men, up to 90 percent of whom came from Chad and Sudan and therefore constituted a foreign invasion force in the eyes of many. They did not speak the local language and are Muslim in a nation that is over 80 percent Christian or otherwise non-Muslim. They destroyed churches, executed priests, stirred up sectarian hatreds where little to none had previously existed.

What we began to see happening last November in response to Seleka was a reactionary backlash by anti-balaka or anti-machete self-defense gangs. Since then, retaliatory outrages committed by anti-balaka forces have escalated, and Muslim civilians who had nothing to do with Seleka became targets.

As in the case of Guen, whole neighborhoods in the capital city of Bangui and whole villages have been cleansed of their Muslim populations. As we will hear from our witnesses, there are numerous causes contributing to grievances including a fight to control conflict minerals. Guen, for example, is a mining area and thus there are economic motives that work there as well.

Insofar as conflict can be described as religious on one level, it is also true that religious fervor and dedication provides the greatest hope for peace and reconciliation in the Central African Republic.

Some of you will recall how a few months ago, three great religious leaders came to Washington as well as to New York, the United Nations, especially meeting with people on both sides of the aisle, both chambers, the White House, and U.N. officials. One was a Muslim imam; another, evangelical Christian leader; and a third, a Catholic bishop from Bangui.

Imam Layama, Archbishop Nzapalainga, and Reverand Nicholas Guérékoyame-Gbangou, the three spoke, and I met with them as did so many others and was absolutely impressed, in awe of their fervor to bring peace and reconciliation to their country and to do just like the Christians or Muslims are trying to do against the Boko Haram where we saw recent outrages.

Greg Simpkins and I were in Jos recently, last September, and we met with the imam there as well as the Catholic archbishop who have joined arms and linked hand to hand their communities to say no to the extremism on either side, in that case is Boko Haram. We are seeing the same positive, interreligious dialogue and cooperation occurring again here in CAR.

Finally, I want to relate to you a story about another man of God, someone whom those of you who attended our November hearing will remember and remember well. Two weeks ago was Holy Week, and on Holy Thursday, Bishop Nongo, who testified at our hearing, was visiting an outlying parish along with three of his priests.

The car he was traveling in was stopped on the road by Seleka gunmen whose leader had for a period occupied his city, his parish. He accused Bishop Nongo of having thwarted his plans in working with international peacekeepers. He then sentenced him and the other three priests to execution and death. The gunmen removed his episocopal ring and a large cross he had around his neck, and you might remember when he sat where you sat, Secretary Jackson, he wore that cross around his neck.

The four men were placed in a truck and were then driven north to the border with Chad for the order to be carried out. On the way to the gallows their truck was stopped, again by Seleka gunmen, this time commanded by another warlord who actually knew Bishop Nongo and knew that he was a true humanitarian and a man of peace and knew that the bishop provided for over 35,000 displaced people in his parish. Whether they were parishioners or not, he just cared for them.

He ordered the bishop and the priests freed, and through efforts of international aid organizations and the peacekeepers, they were helicoptered back to his home parish in time for Good Friday. The story really hit home with me and I am sure it will with others who know him.

Here is someone who I and others shared coffee with, we prayed with him, and then we heard him give powerful testimony. And his clarion call to the international community was to get those peace-keepers, besides all of the humanitarian aid and the other things that he said were so desperately needed. He said we need peace-keepers who will stop the carnage and will do it immediately.

So I am grateful that he survived to continue doing his great life-saving and life-enhancing work, but it just underscores the precarious nature of how everyone, Muslims, Christians, are at risk. Clergy, imam, bishop, they are all at risk in the CAR and we need to redouble our efforts.

And again I thank our witnesses for being here. I yield to my friend and colleague Karen Bass for any opening comments she might have.

Ms. BASS. Thank you, Chairman Smith. As always, thank you for your leadership of this subcommittee and also convening this hearing on the Central African Republic and the prospects that the ongoing conflicts there might intensify into genocide.

I would also like to thank our distinguished witnesses including Ambassador Jackson and Anne Richards from the U.S. Department of State as well as a range of experts from prominent nongovernmental development and advocacy organizations.

I look forward to hearing your perspectives on the ongoing crisis in the Central African Republic including getting an update on the humanitarian situation and the U.S. and international efforts to address the challenges, including the collaboration with the African Union and what is ultimately at stake if efforts to quell the conflict are not implemented with sufficient resources and all deliberate speed.

In April I had the honor of traveling to Rwanda, Burundi, and the Central African Republic as part of the presidential delegation to the region to attend the 20th anniversary of the Rwandan genocide. And while on the Central African Republic leg of the journey, I witnessed firsthand much of the poverty, the chaos, and the lack of economic opportunities which in many ways we know gave rise to much of the current conflict.

In addition to attending the Rwandan genocide memorial, when we went to the CAR it is my understanding in traveling with Ambassador Power that it was the first time a Cabinet-level official had ever traveled to the nation. We met with a group of Muslims and Christians and it was really just tragic to hear their testimonies and their stories.

There was one woman who spoke with us and talked about how she lost both of her children. Her son left that afternoon to go to the market and never came home, and her daughter was later found murdered. And she was a Muslim woman who was now afraid to leave her house.

And Mr. Chairman, you have on many occasions on the human rights portfolio part of the subcommittee talked about the persecution of Christians, and here we have a situation where there is Christian-led militia that are attacking the Muslim population, and in fact it is reported that over 90 percent of the population has been driven out of the country which is a situation that we are certainly going to have to be looking at, how we bring them back in.

When we met with the President of the CAR, even she talked about even how her own security was not stable. I mean, she was frightened. You remember that because there are many of you here who are going to give testimony today were a part of that delegation, and listening to her talk about her own situation was quite frightening.

But we do know that while much as been made of the religious layers of the conflict, the differences in religious ideology were not the origin of the crisis which actually reflects complex tensions over access to resources, control over trade and land, and issues of national identity.

And you certainly when you had the hearing and talked about the religious leaders that were here is an example of how we know that people there and leadership there really do want to resolve this situation in a peaceful way.

So as we prepare to hear from today's witnesses, I hope we can learn critical lessons from the vast experience and use them to increase support by the most effective measures to bring an end to the conflicts in the Central African Republic.

And when we do listen to the witnesses, I am hoping that you will provide guidance for us in terms of if there is anything else that we can do in Congress. So as always I am committed to working toward this end and look forward to working with my colleagues in Washington and on the continent to find a peaceful resolution.

Mr. SMITH. I thank my good friend for her very eloquent statement. And to underscore, as I tried to do in my opening statement, what we have tried to do in this human rights subcommittee, and I have chaired it beginning in 1995—was out of it for a little while, when I did another chairmanship—but let me just say clear and unambiguously, any sectarian violence is to be abhorred, condemned, fought against, struggled against, and what I have tried to do is to emphasize—and I held all the hearings on Srebrenica as that was happening and immediately thereafter when Muslims were targeted simply because they were Muslims—and try to make very clear today that both sides of extremism that are slaughtering people because of their religious faith or ethnicity are to be condemned and held to account.

And just parenthetically I would say to my colleagues, yesterday this committee approved a resolution I have been pushing since September to create a war crimes tribunal that would mirror the great work that was done by David Crane in the Sierra Leone War Crimes Tribunal, Rwanda, and Yugoslavia, an ad hoc tribunal that would go after both sides, those that are killing Christians and those that are killing Muslims and everyone else who is doing the slaughtering in Syria.

I would like to yield to my friend and colleague, Mr. Weber, the vice chairman of the subcommittee.

Mr. WEBER. Thank you, Mr. Chairman. I appreciate you holding this hearing. I am ready to get going and anxious to hear witnesses.

Mr. SMITH. Okay. Mr. Marino?

Okay, I would like to introduce our distinguished witnesses, again thank them for being here, beginning first with Ambassador Robert Jackson, currently the Principal Deputy Assistant Secretary in the Bureau of African Affairs, previously served as the Ambassador to the Cameroon, the deputy chief of mission and Charge d'Affaires at the U.S. Embassies in Morocco and Senegal.

He has also worked in Burundi, Zimbabwe, Portugal, and Canada. At the State Department he has worked in commercial and consular sections and has done officer training. He performed oversight in the Office of the Promotion of Democracy and Human Rights after 9/11, and without objection his full testimony will be made a part of the record.

Ms. Anne Richard who is the Assistant Secretary in the State Department's Population, Refugees, and Migration Bureau, a position she has held since 2012, Ms. Richard's previous government service includes time in the State Department, the Peace Corps, and the Office of Management and Budget. She has also worked at the Council on Foreign Relations, the International Rescue Committee, and was part of the team that founded the International Crisis Group, a group that we hear from often on this committee as well.

So Mr. Ambassador, if you could begin.

STATEMENT OF THE HONORABLE ROBERT P. JACKSON, PRINCIPAL DEPUTY ASSISTANT SECRETARY, BUREAU OF AFRICAN AFFAIRS, U.S. DEPARTMENT OF STATE

Ambassador JACKSON. Thank you very much Chairman Smith, Ranking Member Bass, other members of the subcommittee, for this opportunity to testify again about the Central African Republic (CAR). Since I last appeared before you we have grown more concerned with the interreligious violence that continues between anti-balaka and ex-Seleka militia throughout the Central African Republic.

The United States remains committed to working with the CAR's transitional authorities and the international community to end the violence and build a transitional process leading to the establishment of a legitimate elected government in CAR.

In the process of forcibly taking political power from former CAR President Francois Bozize, Seleka destroyed the traditionally amicable relationship between CAR's Christians and Muslims. Seleka fighters were little more than mercenaries, bandits, and criminals who sustained themselves by looting, killing, kidnapping, and pillaging the country which is 85 to 90 percent Christian and animist.

While the Seleka rebellion did not begin as a religiously-based movement intent on targeting Christians, the disproportionate impact of its extreme violence on the population led to the establishment of Christian self-defense militias, the anti-balaka. These militias then began to engage in revenge killings, first against Seleka rebels then against presumed Seleka supporters, and then indiscriminately against Muslims and their religious sites.

Interim President Djotodia's January 10 resignation occurred only after his rule had bankrupted the government and left a path of destruction and lawlessness that pervades the entire country today. U.N. agencies and human rights organizations have estimated that over 600,000 persons have been displaced since the beginning of the Seleka rebellion in late 2012.

Just since December 2013, at least 2,000 people have been killed, and another 100,000 have fled the country. We are particularly concerned that the imminent threat against Muslim civilians has forced many to abandon their homes and communities and to seek help from U.N. humanitarian agencies, the African Union, and the French peacekeeping forces to relocate within the Central African Republic or to neighboring countries.

Just last weekend, at the urgent request of Muslim civilians in the PK12 neighborhood of Bangui, peacekeeping forces transported over 1,200 people to towns in the northern part of the country. As soon as those folks departed, the remaining local population attacked and destroyed the mosque and looted the homes of those who had left.

This forced relocation of Muslims from their homes and communities is deeply disturbing and fundamentally alters the religious composition and character of CAR's towns and regions. The violence unleashed by Seleka and then compounded by the anti-balaka militias may have permanently changed CAR's historic tradition of religious tolerance and coexistence.

In Bangui alone, an estimated 5,000 to 7,000 Muslims remain out of an estimated previous population of approximately 100,000, and only five of the 37 mosques are still standing. My colleague Anne Richard, Assistant Secretary of State for Population, Refugees, and Migration, traveled to Bangui on April 7. I will defer to her for additional comments about the humanitarian conditions she witnessed and our humanitarian response.

If you will allow me, I would like to explain just what the U.S. Government has done over the past month since her visit to address and stem the communal violence. On April 8th, the U.S. Special Envoy to the Organization of Islamic Cooperation Rashad Hussain and the Department of State's Senior Advisor on CAR David Brown, who is here today, led an interfaith delegation of religious leaders from the United States to demonstrate solidarity among religious communities and promote reconciliation.

In a show of support for this reconciliation, interfaith participants from the CAR, as well as representatives from the government, civil society, and armed groups, signed a communique renouncing violence and encouraging intercommunity and interreligious dialogue to mitigate tensions and lay the foundation for renewed peaceful coexistence.

On April 9, Ambassador to the United Nations Samantha Power and Assistant Secretary of State for African Affairs Linda Thomas-Greenfield, made their second visit to the CAR in a span of 4 months. Ranking Member Bass participated in the delegation's visit and witnessed firsthand the dire conditions in the country.

During their visit, Ambassador Power, Assistant Secretary Thomas-Greenfield and Representative Bass met with transitional President Catherine Samba-Panza, commanders of the 7,000-strong African Union and French peacekeeping forces, and members of civil society to express our continued and unwavering determination to end the violence and support, the reestablishment of legitimate government.

We pledged to work with the government and the international community to help her administration. In response to her request, we will specifically work to reestablish local law enforcement, transitional justice, and accountability capabilities to end impunity which has contributed to continued violence against civilians.

We are pleased that several countries in the region, the World Bank, the European Union, and other development partners have come forward to help finance basic government services and support alternative work programs that will help put CAR citizens back to work.

While we commend the leadership of the African Union and the efforts of the African Union MISCA force with support from the French, we also agree with U.N. Secretary General Ban Ki-moon's assessment that a U.N. peacekeeping force with both military and civilian components is needed to address the crisis in a comprehensive way.

On April 10, the United States joined the other members of the U.N. Security Council in unanimously adopting Resolution 2149 which establishes the U.N. peacekeeping operation in the Central African Republic, known as MINUSCA, with up to 10,000 military personnel, 1,800 police, and 20 corrections officers.

MINUSCA will build on the strong work and sacrifice made by MISCA and the French forces as well as the European troops that are in the process of joining them in the CAR. MINUSCA will have the responsibility not only to protect civilians but also to support the reestablishment of governance, election preparations, disarmament and demobilization of combatants, protection of human rights, and accountability for human rights abuses.

The United States will continue to reinforce the MISCA mission in advance of the transition to MINUSCA in September to maintain and increase MISCA's ability to protect the civilian population. We have committed up to $100 million to support MISCA including by providing airlift to over 1,700 peacekeepers to date, nonlethal equipment, and 200 additional vehicles. Thirty-seven vehicles have already been delivered to increase the ability of troops on the ground.

On April 10, the United States also announced additional humanitarian assistance to the CAR, bringing our humanitarian assistance since October 1, 2013, to $67 million. To support the essential work of reconciliation and peace building, we have committed an additional $7.5 million to nongovernmental organizations to support their courageous work with CAR's religious leaders who are promoting conflict resolution initiatives to encourage peace, forgiveness, and nonviolence in flashpoint areas of the country.

We strongly believe that it is important to hold accountable all individuals responsible for atrocities being committed, and we are actively working with the United Nations Security Council to implement targeted sanctions against political spoilers and the individuals perpetrating the violence. As Secretary of State Kerry stated, the United States is prepared to implement targeted sanctions against those who further destabilize the situation or pursue their own selfish ends by abetting or encouraging violence.

Finally, I am pleased to announce that the Department of State has appointed Ambassador Stuart Symington as our Special Representative for the Central African Republic. He will begin his work later this month. Ambassador Symington will play a leading role in shaping and coordinating U.S. strategy toward the CAR to end the violence, addressing humanitarian needs, establishing legitimate governance, creating judicial mechanisms for ensuring accountability for those suspected of perpetrating human rights abuses, and helping the CAR move through an inclusive transition process leading to democratic elections.

Chairman Smith, Ranking Member Bass, and other members of the subcommittee, we are determined and committed to ending the human suffering in CAR and supporting a peaceful and durable resolution to the crisis. We remain engaged with our international partners, and we look forward to keeping you and the committee engaged and informed of our efforts. I would be pleased to answer your questions. Thank you very much.

[The prepared statement of Ambassador Jackson follows:]

Testimony of Acting Assistant Secretary Robert P. Jackson

Bureau of African Affairs, U.S. Department of State

House Foreign Affairs Committee

Subcommittee on Africa, Global Health, Global Human Rights, and International Organizations

May 1, 2014

Thank you very much Chairman Smith, ranking member Bass, and other Members of the Committee for the opportunity to testify again before you today on this critical issue. Since I last appeared before you on November 19, we have grown more concerned with the inter-religious violence that continues between the anti-Balaka and ex-Seleka militia throughout the Central African Republic (CAR). The United States remains committed to working with the CAR Transitional Authorities and the international community to end the violence and build a transitional process leading to the establishment of a legitimate, elected government in CAR.

Since my previous testimony before you last November, Seleka leader and former CAR Interim President Michel Djotodia was forced to resign and a new transitional president, Catherine Samba-Panza, was selected. However, Djotodia's January 10 departure from office occurred only after his rule had bankrupted the government and left a path of destruction and lawlessness that pervades the entire country today. UN agencies and human rights organizations have estimated that at least 2,000 people have been killed since December and hundreds of thousands displaced since the beginning of the Seleka rebellion in late 2012.

The Seleka rebels, in the process of forcibly taking political power from former CAR President François Bozize, destroyed the traditionally amicable relationship between CAR Christians and Muslims. The Seleka armed group grew with the incorporation of foreign mercenaries, who were little more than opportunistic bandits and criminals who sustained themselves by looting, killing, kidnapping, and pillaging the CAR population, a majority of whom is Christian.

While the Seleka rebellion did not begin as a religiously-based movement intent on destroying Christian believers, the disproportionate impact of its extreme violence on the majority Christian population led to the establishment of Christian self-defense militias, known as anti-Balaka (meaning anti-machete). These anti-Balaka militias then began to engage in revenge killings first against Seleka rebels, then against presumed Seleka supporters, and then indiscriminately against Muslim civilians and Muslim religious sites.

We are particularly concerned that the imminent threat against Muslim civilians has forced many to abandon their homes and communities and seek help from UN humanitarian agencies and the African Union and French peacekeeping forces to relocate elsewhere within CAR or to neighboring countries. Just last weekend, at the urgent request of Muslim civilians in the PK12 neighborhood of Bangui, peacekeeping forces transported about 1,200 people to towns in the northern part of CAR. As soon as they departed, the remaining local population attacked and destroyed the mosque and looted the homes of those who had left. This forced removal of Muslims from their homes and communities is deeply disturbing and fundamentally alters the religious composition and character of CAR's towns and regions.

The violence unleashed by the Seleka rebellion, and then compounded by the anti-Balaka militias, may have permanently changed CAR's historic tradition of religious tolerance and coexistence. In Bangui alone, for example, an estimated 5,000 – 7,000 Muslims remain out of a previous population of nearly 100,000, and only five of 37 mosques are still standing.

We are determined and committed to end the human suffering in CAR and support a peaceful and durable resolution to the crisis in CAR. On April 9, Ambassador to the United Nations Samantha Power and Assistant Secretary of State for African Affairs Linda Thomas-Greenfield made their second visit to CAR in a span of four months. Ranking Member Karen Bass participated in the delegation's visit to CAR and witnessed firsthand the dire situation in that country. During their visit, Ambassador Power, Assistant Secretary Thomas-Greenfield, and Representative Bass met with Transitional President Samba-Panza, commanders of the African Union and French peacekeeping forces, and members of civil society to express our continued and unwavering determination to end the violence and support the reestablishment of legitimate governance. We pledged to work with Transitional President Samba-Panza and the international community to help her administration as it addresses the enormous tasks of bringing peace and security and restoring governance to CAR. In response to her request, we will specifically work with the international community to help reestablish local law enforcement, transitional justice, and accountability capabilities to end impunity, which has contributed to continued violence against civilians.

We also pledged to work with the CAR transitional government and international community to help establish governing institutions and provide basic services. The government is currently bankrupt and unable to pay civil servants' or military salaries. We are pleased that several countries in the region, the World Bank, the European Union, and other development partners have come forward to help finance basic government services and support alternative work programs that will help put CAR citizens back to work.

We continue to work with the international community to reestablish security and protect civilians in CAR. On April 10, the United States joined the other members of the UN Security Council in unanimously adopting Resolution 2149, which establishes a UN peacekeeping operation in CAR, known as MINUSCA. While we commend the leadership of the African Union, and the efforts of the African Union MISCA force, with support from the French, we also agree with UN Secretary General Ban Ki-moon on the need for a UN peacekeeping force with both military and civilian components to address the crisis in a comprehensive way.

UN Security Council Resolution 2149 authorizes MINUSCA to have up to 10,000 military personnel, 1,800 police personnel, and 20 corrections officers. MINUSCA will build on the strong work and sacrifice made by the MISCA and French forces, as well as the European troops that are in the process of joining them in CAR. MINUSCA will have the responsibility not only to protect civilians and establish a safe environment for delivery of humanitarian assistance, but also to help support the reestablishment of governance, assist in election preparations, facilitate the disarmament and demobilization of combatants, assist in reconciliation, promote and protect human rights, and support the formation of accountability mechanisms for those responsible for human rights abuses.

The United States will continue to reinforce the MISCA mission in advance of its transition into MINUSCA in September to maintain and increase its ability to protect the civilian population. We have committed up to $100 million to support MISCA, including by providing airlift for over 1,700 Rwandan and Burundian troops, providing non-lethal equipment, and procuring approximately 200 vehicles, in addition to the 37 we recently delivered, to increase the mobility of the troops on the ground.

We strongly believe it is important to hold accountable all individuals responsible for atrocities being committed in CAR, and we are actively working with the UN Security Council to implement targeted sanctions against political spoilers and those individuals perpetrating the violence in CAR. As Secretary Kerry previously stated, the United States is prepared to implement targeted sanctions against those who further destabilize the situation, or pursue their own selfish ends by abetting or encouraging the violence.

We are also continuing to work to address the suffering of the CAR population. The humanitarian situation in CAR remains dire, with over 628,000 individuals internally displaced and over 112,000 who have fled to neighboring countries since December 2013. Violence continues to beset interior areas of CAR, resulting in humanitarian needs that exceed the capacity of relief agencies to respond. In recent days, armed groups have launched multiple attacks in remote areas.

On April 10, the United States announced an additional $22 million in humanitarian assistance to CAR in recognition of the increased difficulty many will face with the onset of the rainy season there. This additional funding brings our humanitarian assistance total to nearly $67 million this fiscal year. My colleague Anne Richard, Assistant Secretary of State for Population, Refugees and Migration (PRM), traveled to Bangui on April 7. I will defer to her for additional information about the humanitarian conditions in CAR and our response.

To support the essential work of reconciliation and peace building, we have committed $7.5 million to NGOs to support the work of courageous CAR religious leaders who are promoting conflict resolution initiatives to encourage peace, forgiveness, and non-violence in flashpoint areas of the country.

On April 8, U.S. Special Envoy to the Organization of Islamic Cooperation Rashad Hussain and the Department of State's Senior Advisor on CAR David Brown led an interfaith delegation of religious leaders from the United States to demonstrate solidarity among religious communities and promote reconciliation in CAR. Together, U.S. and CAR religious leaders met with Transitional President Samba-Panza to discuss bringing an end to the violence in CAR. They also visited a mosque and a Catholic church in Bangui and participated in joint meetings with Seleka and anti-Balaka representatives and youth leaders. In a show of support for reconciliation, inter-faith participants from CAR, as well as representatives from the CAR government, civil society, and armed groups, signed a communiqué renouncing violence and encouraging intercommunity and interreligious dialogue to mitigate tensions and lay the foundation for renewed peaceful coexistence in CAR.

I am pleased to announce that the Department has appointed Ambassador Stuart Symington as our Special Representative for the CAR, beginning the latter part of this month. Ambassador Symington will play a leading role in shaping and coordinating U.S. strategy toward the CAR to end the violence, address humanitarian needs, establish legitimate governance, create judicial mechanisms for ensuring accountability for those suspected of perpetrating human rights abuses, and help CAR move through an inclusive political transition process leading to democratic elections.

Representative Smith, Ranking Member Bass, and Members of the subcommittee, let me assure you that we continue to remain engaged with our international partners to address the crisis in CAR. We look forward to keeping you and the subcommittee informed of our efforts. I hope this information is helpful to the subcommittee. I am glad to answer any questions you might have.

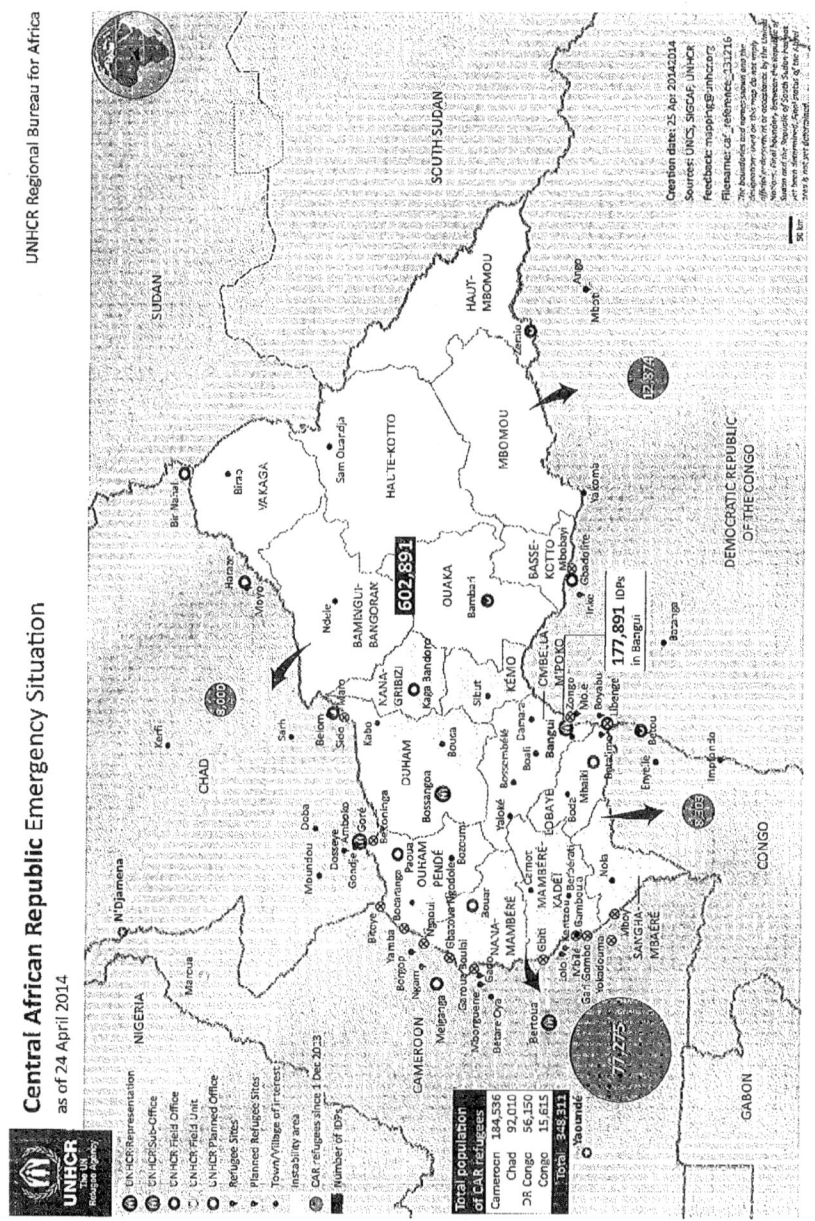

Mr. SMITH. Ambassador Jackson, thank you very much for your testimony and for your work. It is all appreciated.

I would like to now yield to Assistant Secretary Anne Richard for her testimony.

STATEMENT OF THE HONORABLE ANNE RICHARD, ASSISTANT SECRETARY, BUREAU OF POPULATION, REFUGEES AND MIGRATION, U.S. DEPARTMENT OF STATE

Ms. RICHARD. Thank you very much, Mr. Chairman, Ranking Member Bass, other members of the subcommittee, and thank you throughout the year for your dedication to human rights and humanitarian causes. We greatly appreciate that. And I appreciate the opportunity today to brief you on the humanitarian crisis in the Central African Republic.

As you said, it is unusual to have two witnesses from the State Department, but because I was just in Bangui at the beginning of April we thought it might make sense to come along and provide some eyewitness testimony from what I saw on that trip.

Principal Deputy Assistant Secretary Jackson has provided you with a comprehensive overview of the situation, so I want to focus on my remarks on the travel that I had at the beginning of April to Chad and also to Bangui, Central African Republic on April 7. And I want to highlight the work that the Bureau of Population, Refugees, and Migration is doing, and also we are doing that together with U.S. Agency for International Development to address humanitarian needs.

As you know, nearly 1 million Central Africans have been forced to flee their homes, two-thirds are displaced within the Central African Republic, and one-third have fled to neighboring countries and thus are now refugees, and many of them have fled since last December. Each and every one of these uprooted people has stories of personal tragedy and loss including family members killed, wives and children raped and abused, and dreams shattered.

In Chad, I traveled to the south to areas near the border with the Central African Republic and also toward a transit center in N'Djamena. I spoke with one Muslim man who showed me photos of the mutilated body of his father. The parents of five children, including a newborn baby, told me they had lost everything, and people have brought very little with them and some were using what little they had to build very rudimentary shelters to house their families.

I travel a lot to refugee situations, to displaced persons' camps. People were in very difficult shelter situations and it was, obviously they were in places that had been thrown together very quickly and they were safe for the moment, but it was certainly, what I saw was nothing for people to live in for any length of time.

In Bangui, CAR, I spoke to several women, all Christians and all living in extremely difficult conditions with their children at the M'Poko airport internally displaced persons site. And as you may have seen, Ranking Member Bass, the IDP site is right there on the edge of the airport so we didn't have to travel far to meet with them.

While their homes were in a nearby neighborhood they all sought protection at the IDP camp because they were afraid that if they went back to their homes they could be hurt in the crossfire, in the violence, and the gunfire. In all my meetings, security was the number one topic of concern. From Cabinet Ministers to U.N. leaders to refugees and internally displaced persons themselves, all spoke of the need to restore security and a sense of law and order in the country.

And this is the number one message I want to bring to you today is because we heard it unanimously from everyone, was that they were concerned about the violence. When I asked refugees why they had fled, they all mentioned fear of attack and concern for their families. In Bangui, the Minister of Rural Development said she had a program to distribute seeds to farmers, but the program would be worthless if farmers did not feel safe enough to plant their fields.

I cannot reiterate strongly enough the importance of robust U.S. Government support to the African Union's stabilization mission in CAR, MISCA, and the new U.N. integrated mission in CAR, MINUSCA. The restoration of security is essential to creating conditions that will one day permit these 1 million uprooted people to return home.

Meanwhile, the U.S. Government is committed to working with the international community to provide lifesaving assistance inside CAR and in neighboring countries and to structure our aid programs to enhance efforts to protect the displaced.

During my visit to Chad I was particularly struck by the incredible hospitality of the Chadian people and their government. They had not only opened their doors to 92,000 Central African refugees, but were also welcoming the return of an equal number of Chadian migrants who had been living in the Central African Republic for decades but were no longer safe in the country.

I know this same degree of hospitality has been extended by the Democratic Republic of the Congo, the Republic of the Congo, and especially Cameroon which now hosts the largest number of refugees from the Central African Republic at 184,000.

And the other point to make about Chad as you all well know is that they have for over a decade hosted refugees from Darfur, so they already had many refugees living in the country. I was also tremendously impressed by the dedication and commitment of relief workers who at great risk to themselves were struggling to gain access to vulnerable populations to deliver aid including food, water, shelter, and health care.

Sadly, relief workers too have lost their lives including three people working with Médecins Sans Frontières who were killed this past weekend in northwest Central African Republic. They were simply trying to deliver health care.

In Chad, newly arriving refugees were receiving only half of the recommended daily food ration because World Food Programme resources are stretched so thin. Several refugees approached me personally and told me that they did not have enough food to feed their children and they were very concerned about that.

And I have to say that that doesn't usually happen when I travel to refugee camps. Usually if people have reached a refugee camp they are safe and they are cared for. In this particular case, I talked to the World Food Programme about it and they said they knew that the food was under the recommended levels and they did not blame the United States. They said the United States had been generous but that the other countries had not come through with their shares.

In CAR, conditions in the IDP camp at the Bangui airport were deplorable in terms of overcrowding. Shelter was poor. International nongovernmental organizations in partnership with local authorities were doing their best to address gaps. It is clear to me that the nearly $67 million the U.S. Government through the PRM Bureau and also through USAID have provided so far this year is money well-invested. Our work is certainly not over.

Since my return, the Office of the U.N. High Commissioner for Refugees found it necessary to take the extraordinary step of evacuating the last Muslim population from Bossangoa and taking them to Chad, essentially helping them to become refugees, and we are not normally in the business of turning people into refugees. We normally try to prevent that situation from occurring. Others in Bangui have been evacuated to safer spots inside CAR. These are extraordinary steps and they were not taken lightly. It was done to avoid massacres, frankly, and so very much as a last resort measure.

On April 16, the United Nations released its 2014 Central African Republic Regional Response Plan which calls for $274 million to address the crisis. We will review both appeals and provide additional funding in the near future. Thanks to Congress, and this is a very important point, thanks to Congress we have appropriations to do more this year, but as you know we are contending with too many humanitarian emergencies. Unrest in the Central African Republic is happening at the same time as upheaval and violence in South Sudan. Secretary Kerry is in meetings today in Addis about South Sudan and widespread conflict in Syria.

While humanitarian funding will certainly help keep people alive, let me again remind you of the plea made by refugees and IDPs during my recent visit. Above all else they wanted a return to security and stability in the Central African Republic. They wanted conditions that would permit them to return home, rebuild their lives, rebuild their homes, go back to work in their places of business. This should be our highest priority as well.

Representative Smith, Ranking Member Bass, and members of the subcommittee, I thank you for your support and for giving me the opportunity to address you today and I am happy to answer your questions.

[The prepared statement of Ms. Richard follows:]

Testimony of Assistant Secretary Anne C. Richard

Bureau of Population, Refugees, and Migration, U.S. Department of State

House Foreign Affairs Committee

Subcommittee on African Affairs

May 1, 2014

Mr. Chairman, Ranking Member Bass, and Members of the Subcommittee:

I greatly appreciate this opportunity today to brief you on the humanitarian crisis in the Central African Republic (CAR) and its spillover into neighboring countries. Principal Deputy Assistant Secretary Jackson has just provided you with a comprehensive overview of the situation in CAR and the efforts the United States government has made, working with the international community, to end the violence and help CAR move beyond this current nightmare. I would like to focus my remarks on my recent travel to Chad from April 1st through 6th and to Bangui, CAR on April 7th, and I want to highlight the work that the Bureau of Population, Refugees, and Migration (PRM) is doing – in coordination with our colleagues at the U.S. Agency for International Development – to address the humanitarian needs of Central Africans and others affected by the crisis.

To set the stage, let me first share with you a few sobering statistics on population displacement. Nearly one million Central Africans have been forced to flee their homes. Nearly two-thirds [603,000] are displaced within CAR while one-third [348,000] have fled to neighboring countries and thus are now refugees. They have fled to Chad (92,000), Cameroon (184,000), the Democratic Republic of the Congo (56,000), and the Republic of Congo (16,000).

Beyond numbers, each and every one of these uprooted people have stories of personal tragedy and loss, including family members killed, wives and children raped and abused, and dreams shattered.

In Chad, I traveled to the South, to areas near the border with CAR, and also toured a transit center in N'djamena. I spoke with one Muslim man who showed me photos of the mutilated body of his father. The parents of five children – including a newborn baby – told me they had lost everything. People had brought very little with them and some were using what little they had to build very rudimentary shelters to house their families.

In Bangui, CAR, I spoke to several women, all Christians and all living in extremely difficult conditions with their children at the M'Poko Airport internally displaced persons (IDP) site. While their homes were in a nearby neighborhood, they all sought protection at the IDP camp, fearing attack by armed gunmen who continued to shoot civilians.

In all my meetings, security was the number one topic of concern. From Cabinet ministers in the transitional Central African government to UN leaders to the refugees and internally displaced persons, all spoke of the need to restore security and a sense of law and order in the country. When I asked refugees why they had fled, they all mentioned fear of attack and concern for their families. In Bangui, the Minister of Rural Development said she had a program to distribute seeds to farmers, but the program would be worthless if farmers did not feel safe enough to plant their fields.

I cannot reiterate strongly enough the importance of robust U.S. government support to the African Union's Stabilization Mission in CAR (MISCA) and the new United Nations integrated mission in CAR (MINUSCA). The restoration of security is essential to creating conditions that will one day permit these one million uprooted persons to return home.

Meanwhile, the U.S. Government is committed to working with the international community to provide life-saving assistance inside CAR and in neighboring countries and to structuring our aid programs to enhance efforts to protect the displaced. During my visit to Chad, I was particularly struck by the incredible hospitality of the Chadian people and their government. They had not only opened their doors to 92,000 Central African refugees but were also welcoming the return of an equal number of Chadian migrants who had been living in CAR for decades but were no longer safe in the country. I know this same degree of hospitality has been extended by the Democratic Republic of the Congo, the Republic of Congo, and especially Cameroon which now hosts the largest number of CAR refugees at 184,000.

I was also tremendously impressed by the dedication and commitment of relief workers who, at great risk to themselves, were struggling to gain access to vulnerable populations to deliver humanitarian aid including food, water, shelter, and health care. Sadly, many relief workers have lost their lives, including three people working with Medecins sans Frontieres (or Doctors Without Borders) who were killed this past weekend in Northwest CAR. They were simply trying to deliver health care.

In Chad, newly arriving refugees were receiving only half of the recommended daily food ration because World Food Program resources are stretched so thin. Several approached me to tell me that they were not getting enough food to feed their children. In CAR, conditions in the IDP camp at the Bangui airport were deplorable in terms of overcrowding and shelter was poor. However, international and non-governmental organizations, in partnership with local authorities, were doing their best to address gaps. It was clear to me that the nearly $67 million the U.S. government – through PRM and USAID – has provided so far in Fiscal Year 2014 to support the efforts of international and non-governmental organizations to meet the needs of Central African internally displaced persons and refugees has been money well spent.

Our work is certainly not over. Since my return, the Office of the United Nations High Commissioner for Refugees (UNHCR) found it necessary to take the extraordinary step of evacuating the last Muslim population from Bossangoa and taking them to Chad – essentially helping them to become refugees. Others in Bangui have been evacuated to safer spots inside CAR. I would stress that these are very unusual steps – considered a measure of last resort that reflects the gravity of the threats to civilians. These steps are not taken lightly given the possible unintended consequences of further entrenching the separation of religious communities in the CAR, a country which has had a long history of communal tolerance.

On April 16, the United Nations released its 2014 Central African Republic Regional Response Plan, which calls for $274 million to address CAR-related humanitarian needs in Chad, Cameroon, the Democratic Republic of the Congo, and the Republic of Congo, and an updated UN appeal for CAR alone is also anticipated. We will review both appeals and provide additional funding in the near future. Thanks to Congress, we have appropriations to do more this year but, as you know, we are contending with too many humanitarian emergencies. Unrest in CAR is happening at the same time as upheaval and violence in South Sudan and widespread conflict in Syria.

While humanitarian funding will certainly help keep people alive, let me again remind you of the plea made by refugees and IDPs during my recent visit. Above all else, they wanted a return to security and stability in CAR; they wanted conditions that would permit them to return home and rebuild their lives, homes, and places of business. This should be our highest priority as well.

Representative Smith, Ranking Member Bass, and Members of the Subcommittee: I thank you for your support and for giving me the opportunity to speak today. I welcome any questions you may have.

Mr. SMITH. Thank you so very much, Ms. Richard. To begin the questioning just let me ask a number of questions starting with Mr. Ambassador. With regards to peacekeeping, when can we realistically expect peacekeepers to be on the ground displacing those who are being augmented out because of those conflicts that we all know and vested interests that have compromised their mission? Are we talking the fall? And is there any way to accelerate that process? Because delay is denial obviously for those who are being hurt and/or killed.

Let me ask you as well, and maybe this would be to you, Ms. Richard. My understanding is that our humanitarian assistance numbers approximately $67 million. And the question would arise, why are faith-based organizations only getting $7.5 million given the outsize role that they are playing in the Central African Republic?

As we know, when Bishop Nongo was here, he was concerned that he is sheltering 35,000 people. And how much assistance are we giving to those NGOs or faith-based entities that could have high-impact because they know and are understood and respected by the people that they deal with? It seems that that ratio is very much skewed toward not helping faith-based entities, and if you could give some insight into that.

Kasper Agger from Enough makes the point in his testimony that combatants, politicians, businessmen, and diplomats were all giving him the same excuses and reasons for the crisis in the country, lack of leadership and exclusion of citizens. But he also makes the point that—and I thought this was very interesting—that some of the key drivers of violence are the diamonds and the poaching. And if you could speak to that issue and that there is a need for sustained, regional U.S. diplomatic engagement that looks at those aspects of it. How do we dry up those nefarious enterprises?

Let me also ask you as well, Madeline Rose in her testimony points out that if we fail to address CAR's crisis quickly and correctly, Mercy Corps is concerned that the situation could metastasize into a new decades-long conflict transcending the corridor from the Sahel to South Sudan, and makes the point that even with the anticipated EU reinforcements, the enormity of challenge for peacekeepers outstrips capacities.

Is this designed potentially to fail? And I am not assuming any ill will here, but is it being driven by insufficient resources? You just mentioned that other countries have not come through with their commitments. How much of an unmet need do we have with regards to peacekeeping?

What kind of force is needed ideally to really end this violence, and is what is configured enough? Is the money enough? How much are we giving to peacekeeping? What are the others giving? And maybe this one could be for the records, but when you say other countries are not coming through, if there could be a listing of those countries, commitments made, commitments unmet, and there are large numbers of countries that could do a heck of a lot more, I would think, that are not doing it.

And finally, and I will have other questions, but maybe you could start with those and then I will get back.

Ambassador JACKSON. Thank you, Mr. Chairman. As for the U.N. peacekeeping force, we anticipate their arrival in mid-September. However, I want to note that the U.N. has already had senior officials on the ground to do the planning and the coordinating with the African Union and French forces, and European Union troops are beginning to arrive and they have started to train 480 police and gendarmes from Central African Republic.

We are also today having Assistant Secretary Thomas-Greenfield, who is with Secretary Kerry in Addis Ababa, meet with the African Union to discuss the deployment of additional African troops from Burundi and Rwanda. We hope that that will take place very soon and we are positioned to move those troops quickly. These troops would replace the Chadians who withdrew at the end of March.

Mr. SMITH. About how many are we talking about, and what would be the force that would make the difference and are we getting close to that or at that number?

Ambassador JACKSON. Mr. Chairman, I honestly don't know what the force need is. We will be going from 7,000 to about 8,200 with the arrival of these additional troops, assuming that the African Union approves both the Rwandan and Burundi contributions. The EU presence will go from about 100 at present to 500 present so that will bring us up to close to 9,000.

Mr. SMITH. Do military planners at the Pentagon and at the U.N. say that that is a sufficient force with a robust mandate to bring some peace to these people who are suffering?

Ambassador JACKSON. Well, let me answer your question a bit differently, Mr. Chairman. In terms of displaced people in Bangui, we have seen the number decline from 500,000 to 200,000, which is not to suggest that the situation is not atrocious. And the removal of the Muslims and the flight of the Muslims contributes to those numbers, so I don't want to be misleading.

But the fact that the number of internally displaced people in Bangui is declining, I think, shows that MISCA and the French forces are having some impact. And as we get these police and gendarmes trained, we are hopeful that those numbers will be sufficient to restore security. I think we are going to have to look at this on a regular basis and see what progress is being made, but to date the progress is not adequate and we acknowledge that.

As for peacekeeping more broadly, our missions and the U.N. missions in Mali and South Sudan are both under-subscribed. We are in conversations with partners about plussing up those missions as well as contributing to the mission in Central African Republic, but it has been a difficult process to identify capable peacekeepers.

Finally, you spoke about diamonds and poaching. Central African diamond exports are currently suspended under the Kimberley Process, but we are hopeful that as the government can restore authority in combination with the peacekeepers that legal diamond exports can once again start, and this would provide the government with revenue that is needed to pay salaries and provide other basic services.

As for poaching, because of the conflict it is difficult to know how much poaching has taken place, but it is clearly a problem in the

Central African Republic as one of the countries that still has a significant population of elephants to poach.

Mr. SMITH. Thank you.

Ms. RICHARD. On the question of the funding distribution, it is true the U.S. is providing nearly $7.5 million in funding to support conflict mitigation, reconciliation, and peacebuilding including interreligious peacebuilding efforts. I would expect that these efforts would not require as much funding as the type of large-scale humanitarian operations that are being carried out for so many people in the Central African Republic and in the region. All of the neighboring countries are affected.

And in addition, some of the nongovernmental organizations that are responding to humanitarian work are indeed faith-based groups and that includes Catholic Relief Services that is speaking today and that gets funding from the USAID's Office of Foreign Disaster Assistance. And they are on the list of one of the groups that is providing logistic support and relief commodities in the region.

And then in addition, we have several high-level delegations going as you heard, and one of those was an interfaith group from the U.S., so that is additional costs that are not reflected in the $7.5 million. I think we are doing a lot, and I think that some of it is reflected in the funding and some of it is perhaps diplomatic efforts that are within the State Departments base budget.

So we have the $100 million you have heard to support the current peacekeeping. We will support the U.N.'s peacekeepers as we do year in and year out thanks to congressional appropriations. The $67 million in humanitarian assistance working with nongovernmental organizations that are across the country, and I think this network of nongovernmental organizations that are normal partners but that are present in really sort of far-flung locations, hard to reach places across Central African Republic, is very, very important for us.

Working in the neighboring countries, the U.N. is moving people away from threats as you have heard. The high-level visits, Samantha Power going twice but also other groups, our diplomats have participated in all the conferences on the Central African Republic that have taken place in New York, in Brussels, in Africa.

We have now Stu Symington named as the Special Representative. We are looking into having, restoring the diplomatic presence in Bangui and that was also going on during this early April set of visits. And then in addition to that we have this money for conflict mitigation and peacebuilding.

Mr. SMITH. Could you provide us a list of groups that are getting the money, the humanitarian assistance, and what might be anticipated going forward particularly as it relates to faith-based? Because again, I was moved and I am sure the subcommitte was that Bishop Nongo was dealing with so much on an absolute shoestring. And he was not going to let a single person go unhelped even if he didn't have the money.

I mean it was just, and it seems to me we need to be backstopping people that are on the ground, have the credibility, and have a record as he and so many others do, and so I just hope we are not bypassing them unwittingly or for any other reason. So if you could provide that for us that would be very helpful.

Ms. RICHARD. Absolutely. On the issue of other countries not providing funding, the World Food Programme resources are stretched thin, not just in the Central African Republic but in the entire region and it is a very difficult situation. And they are doing so much good work there and also in the Middle East with the Syria crisis too.

So I regularly meet with World Food Programme colleagues. As you know, an American runs the World Food Programme. One of their issues is that the European Union's humanitarians, ECHO, had a cash flow problem, so they will have funding later this year. They will provide it. But you can't go back in time and take that funding to feed people. And so this is an example where a cash-flow problem, which is not unheard of in Washington sometimes, is actually having real damage on the ground. And so that is a shame.

And then the other thing that we would like to do is bring new donors to the table, and we have succeeded in some respects with the Syria crisis in getting Gulf states more involved. But we need more countries to step forward and take up the humanitarian cause and provide funding so that the U.S. share stays at an appropriate level. A robust level, a healthy level thanks to you all, but also that it be a multilateral undertaking.

Finally, you had asked about restoring law and order. I really think in talking to experts that it is not just a matter of peace-keepers, it is also a matter of the police, the judicial system, the prisons. This is not my area, but this is what I heard from people there.

So in coming back, Linda Thomas-Greenfield and I have met with Bill Brownfield who is our counterpart, Assistant Secretary for International Narcotics and Law Enforcement, and we are all working to try to figure out what particular role can the U.S. play, in addition to what other countries are doing, to help ordinary citizens enjoy the basic public safety that they used to enjoy in Bangui and other cities and towns.

Mr. SMITH. Lastly, Mr. Ambassador, you said pre-genocidal stage at your last hearings here. Is it genocidal now?

Ambassador JACKSON. Mr. Chairman, we really haven't considered the question of whether it is genocidal or not. The fact is, horrible atrocities are taking place and we know that at least 2,000 people have died. I don't think it matters what word we use, but the situation is horrible and we are doing everything we can to reverse it.

Mr. SMITH. I appreciate that. I do think it matters but I respect the difference.

Ms. Bass?

Ms. BASS. Alright, I know that there is going to be a call for a vote soon, so we know we will be interrupted, but anyway, I will get started.

I am real concerned about, as I mentioned in my opening comments about the displacement of the Muslim population and essentially the stage that that sets especially for extremists to kind of enter that population. And I believe, Ambassador Jackson, you were talking about the movement of the population toward the north.

So I am wondering if, I mean, I am sure you share those concerns, but if there is any evidence of that becoming problematic in terms of outside forces coming in and trying to take advantage of the fact, the revenge killings that have happened.

Ambassador JACKSON. Congresswoman, we have certainly been looking at the question of outside forces coming in just as the Lord's Resistance Army has come in. To date we have not seen that happening. But this separation of religious communities and de facto partition of the country into Christian and Muslim areas is very troubling, and I believe that the sooner we can restore basic security so that people feel safe returning to their homes, the sooner that we will be able to address this problem and avoid long-term partition and consequences that would come from that.

Ms. BASS. One of the things about Rwanda that was so, just hard to imagine but I know it is one of the reasons why the country has been successful in its development since the genocide, but their whole reconciliation process, the fact that people really live down the street and their neighbors are folks that might have slaughtered members of their family.

And I am just wondering, I was just there for just such a brief time, but if the Rwandans are involved in terms of helping the CAR leadership toward the future of how to have a reconciliation process.

Ambassador JACKSON. I don't know if there have been formal discussions, but one of the reasons we have been so pleased to have Rwanda and Burundi contribute peacekeepers is because of their own history of genocide in both countries. And we believe that the troops can talk with people, engage with people, and encourage them to avoid the conflict that we are seeing.

Ms. BASS. And we did go to Burundi and so certainly had some concerns about what we saw there and what looms there in terms of the election next year. You mentioned the food supply as being below what is needed. And I believe, Ambassador Richard, you said that the U.S. had been generous but other countries had been lacking. And I believe the chairman asked the same question in terms of which countries and dollar amount and whether you can answer it now or not. Is that pretty much what you were asking? I would like to know that information as well, because I am wondering if there are ways that we can step up pressure on those other countries so that they do carry their fair share.

Ms. RICHARD. Well, we can work with the USAID to get you the breakdown of who is contributing to the World Food Programme and specifically in the Central African Republic and in the region. But I want to repeat that one missing partner who is normally there with us are the Europeans, and it is an unusual thing this year that they are having cash flow problems.

So normally, the U.S. and Europe together lead the world in humanitarian response, and other countries that year in and year out step forward including Europeans and the European Union are the Canadians, Australians, New Zealanders, Japan, Korea more and more. Turkey, I met yesterday with the Turkish Ambassador, Turkey is stepping forward to play a larger role as a donor internationally. And then with Syria we see Gulf states stepping forward.

But we would like to see more countries who haven't been traditional donors join us, especially in a year like this one where we have three of what the United Nations call Level 3 emergencies. Syria, South Sudan, and the Central African Republic. And I am proud that our country is doing so much. I am proud when I meet with my counterparts from other countries that I can speak up about how much Americans are doing. But I also think this system only works when other countries join us in these kinds of enterprises.

Ms. BASS. Well, France is certainly playing a leading role. What are they doing in terms of pushing other EU countries?

Ms. RICHARD. France is playing a leading role in the situation in this particular country, and also in terms of the peacekeeping piece of it.

Ms. BASS. Right.

Ms. RICHARD. But they are not leaders necessarily on the humanitarian funding piece, whereas in Brussels they do get credit for contributing to the overall European contributions. But also DFID, the Department for International Development in London is the leading donor as well. Within Europe, the UK is really the top donor, I think, with us on the international stage.

Ms. BASS. So last question. I am wondering about the diaspora that is here and if you feel there might be a role that the diaspora that is here can play. There is a young man in the audience who often comes to the hearings, Yves Kongolo, who is from the Central African Republic and has an NGO. And I often work in the breakfasts and the other programs that we do here on the Hill, work a lot with the diaspora, and I am just wondering if you have any thoughts about how the diaspora here might be helpful there.

Ms. RICHARD. It is a great question. I haven't met with members of the diaspora from the Central African Republic. I regularly meet with diasporas. Syrian-Americans. I met recently with Eritrean-Americans. Because we run the program, response to the program to resettle refugees in the United States, I am regularly meeting with Somalis around the United States, and more and more Iraqis around the United States.

So it would not come as a surprise to any of you that we love working with diasporas, meeting with diasporas, and figuring out ways to bring their talents, connections, ability to message, especially in the case here of messages of peace, reconciliation, stability, tolerance. I think that is a key thing that they could play.

Ms. BASS. Well, maybe you have just described a role that we could play, which is to facilitate that introduction for you. Because I hear all the time of people wanting to play very specific roles exactly like that but also in development. So I will have another group of diaspora for you to meet with.

Ms. RICHARD. Happy to.

Mr. SMITH. Mr. Weber.

Mr. WEBER. Thank you, Mr. Chairman. And I guess this question is for you, Mr. Jackson, or for you, Ms. Richard, either one. The Chadian soldiers that came in and killed, remember, and injured so many. Any identification? Any idea who they are? Any accountability there?

Ambassador JACKSON. Congressman Weber, we don't really know who they are. But we will be looking at the units in terms of Leahy vetting for future training, and the need to look very carefully at the participation of Chadians in future peacekeeping operations based on their conduct in the Central African Republic.

Mr. WEBER. Well, I think long term we need to be sending the signal that that won't be tolerated and somehow there has to be accountability and the perpetrators brought to justice so that there is no recurring incidents of that nature. Any way to put pressure on their government to do that to aid in that?

Ambassador JACKSON. I understand that the Chadian Government is doing an investigation and we will look to ensure that they are held to account for their actions.

Mr. WEBER. I guess unlike the other mall shootings there is no video. There is absolutely no evidence to this, or is that——

Ambassador JACKSON. I am not aware of any video. The only thing that I am aware of are testimonies by some of the victims.

Mr. WEBER. Which one of our agencies coordinates with the Chadian Government to say you have got to do more to bring these perpetrators to justice? Who follows that up?

Ambassador JACKSON. The Department of State does, and specifically our Ambassador-at-Large for War Crimes Issues, Ambassador Rapp, and he has been in the region.

Mr. WEBER. Okay. I was doing a little research on that event, and even Aljazeera, the news organization, said this was an underreported occurrence. I didn't see it. I looked at some of the other news agencies and I actually saw it, but they didn't give it the same coverage. So I think it is imperative for us to keep on the forefront and to keep that pressure on so that those kinds of people know that we won't allow this going forward. I think I remember——

Ms. RICHARD. Congressman?

Mr. WEBER. Yes, ma'am?

Ms. RICHARD. It may have been underreported in the United States. There was a lot of coverage of it in the region, and the reason I know that is because it was still unfolding during our visit. And when I was in Chad they decided to bring their peacekeepers home, and at the same time there was a U.N. report on the incident that came out. So there has been a lot of attention, and these situations are complicated because you don't want peacekeepers abusing people in any way, shape or form. They are there to protect people.

At the same time, we had Chad doing so much to try to restore stability overall and we needed more peacekeepers, not less. So you are absolutely right that you cannot support, we cannot support sending people to a country where they abuse the local people. That is not the purpose at all, and so we have to be vigilant in keeping that from happening in the first place and then holding people accountable when it does happen.

But I do think there is attention being paid to it, and I am sorry we don't have specific answers for you today, and I think we have to stay on top of it.

Mr. WEBER. Okay, thank you. I remember our colleague over here, Ranking Member Bass, I think she said religious differences were not the origin of the conflict. Would you elaborate on what you think is the origin of the conflict?

Ambassador JACKSON. Congressman, this is a country that has had a long tradition of conflict. You will remember that Emperor Bokassa was famous for his cannibalism. This is a country that has had conflicts between grazers and agriculturists. We have seen coup after coup. This is the third time that we have evacuated our Embassy because of unrest in the Central African Republic. There is a long and sad history here. I hope this time that we can do better to get it right so that we don't have another repetition of the unrest.

Mr. WEBER. Some of my research said the former President or Prime Minister bankrupted the country, had a lot of graft, a lot of corruption, and then he was basically was gone. Whatever happened to him? Was there any attempt to hold him accountable?

Ambassador JACKSON. We have actually spoken with former President Bozize, and encouraged him to issue public statements calling for calm. We are looking at his role in the current violence. And again, as my colleague said, we want to hold those accountable for the violence responsible.

Mr. WEBER. Okay. And then I think you all said earlier that— and we are running out of time. I know they have called votes. You are expecting some more peacekeeping forces in mid-September, 480 gendarmes?

Ambassador JACKSON. There are 480 gendarmes. They are Central Africans who are undergoing training at present. I would expect that they would be active long before September.

Mr. WEBER. What does that make the total? You said 7,000 to 8,000?

Ambassador JACKSON. So we are currently at approximately 7,000. We are looking at adding a battalion of Rwandans which would be 850 people. We are looking at adding 400 peacekeepers from Burundi. That would bring the total to about 8,200, plus 500 European troops from various countries would be 8,700 in total, prior to September when the peacekeeping operation would come into effect.

And if I may add, Congressman, I think it is really important to note that while the U.N. peacekeepers are not yet in place some of the troops that are there will transition to the U.N. force. But the U.N. political mission is in place and the deputy is our former Ambassador to the Central African Republic, Ambassador Larry Wohlers.

Mr. WEBER. Okay. In the interest of time I am going to yield back. Thank you.

Mr. SMITH. Mr. Marino?

Mr. MARINO. Thank you. I am going to do a lightning round here. I am not able to come back, I have another commitment. But get your pencils out please, and this should be a matter of record. First of all, why has not the International Criminal Court interceded in here in going after these murderers? Number one.

Number two, you said that the troops will be, U.N. troops will get there in September of this year. Why so long? And I am not saying so long in a pejorative sense because perhaps you can describe the process you have to go through. I do not understand the process, and if anything takes more than 5 minutes for me it is too long. How many U.N. troops will be there? When did these murders start to show up on State's radar and the U.N. as well, I am curious to see, because that goes into my question as why is it taking so long.

Are the Muslim and Christian world leaders, the world leaders of the Muslims and Christians, are they standing up and saying to their religious followers, knock this off, or do they have any role in visiting, or representatives visiting over there telling their religious followers that this will not be tolerated from their religious standpoint?

And since 1996, the DRC, it has been embroiled in violence. Over 5.4 million people have been killed. That is something that just does not take place over a year. It has taken place over years, and my question is, why not long before this? And with that I yield back.

Ambassador JACKSON. So I will try to respond very quickly. We have become very aware of the murders since November and December, and that is when the bulk of the violence has taken place. In terms of the movement of the U.N. peacekeepers, the recruitment is what takes so long. One of the reasons that the State Department and the U.S. Government supported the standing up the African Union force was precisely because they could deploy faster than the U.N. and since we are seeing a roughly 6-month timetable for U.N. deployment, I think that our conclusion that we needed to get the African troops in place was the right one.

But it is very important to make this transition to a force that will have roughly 8,000 troops soon to almost 12,000 in September, assuming we can find additional peacekeepers. And the religious leaders from various countries including the Holy See are taking an active role.

Foreign Ministers of Turkey and Guinea were just in Central African Republic this week talking with religious leaders. The Organization of the Islamic Conference Special Envoy, the former Foreign Minister of Senegal, Cheikh Tidiane Gadio, was there with them. We believe that the religious leaders are working well with their counterparts in Central African Republic and doing what they can to appease the situation.

Mr. MARINO. But don't you think it would be beneficial if the religious leaders came out on an international level and made these statements?

Ambassador JACKSON. I do think it would be useful. And just as we broadcast President Obama's message to Central Africans in December, I think having messages from world religious leaders could be useful and it is something that we have been discussing as we bring religious leaders to visit Central African Republic.

Mr. SMITH. Thank you. Can I just ask you—we are out of time on this vote, but what role, if any, has the Atrocities Prevention Board played? Again, I mean we have all been raising issues. You have been raising this. Have they been AWOL or have they been very much a part of the effort to try to prevent and now resolve this?

Ambassador JACKSON. Mr. Chairman, the Atrocities Prevention Board has met. Their most recent meeting was looking at Nigeria and Burundi. But there have been regular meetings and we have been working hand in hand to make certain——

Mr. SMITH. They met on CAR?

Ambassador JACKSON. I haven't seen the agenda for all the meetings, but I believe—I can get back to you on that.

Mr. SMITH. Would you get back to us? Because we certainly haven't heard any outcomes document or any recommendations from them. I am just wondering what role they have played. Because it was stood up with great fanfare as I said in my opening, and it certainly has a great deal of promise. Is that promise being met?

Ambassador JACKSON. Mr. Chairman?

Mr. SMITH. Yes.

Ambassador JACKSON. I apologize. My colleague just advised that there has been at least one APB meeting on Central African Republic.

Mr. SMITH. Do you know what their recommendations were?

Ambassador JACKSON. I do not, but I will get back to you.

Mr. SMITH. Because it would seem that people like yourself, you should at least know what this group is recommending. Thank you.

We stand in brief recess. I do have a number of other questions but the vote precludes that. A brief recess and then we will come back to our second panel. And thank you so very much.

[Recess.]

Mr. SMITH. The subcommittee will reconvene, and I want to apologize to all of our very distinguished witnesses for that delay. We did have a series of votes. There was no way we could cut that any shorter.

I would like to begin with our second panel and beginning first with Mr. Scott Campbell, who is the Catholic Relief Services regional director for Central Africa. He coordinates CRS programs in Burundi, Cameroon, Chad, Central African Republic, and the Democratic Republic of the Congo, the Republic of Congo, and Rwanda.

Since joining CRS, Mr. Campbell has coordinated food aid during the Kosovo crisis, overseen the emergency response to the 2004 tsunami in the northern Indonesian province of Aceh, and directed CRS's response to the 2010 earthquake in Haiti. He also served as CRS's county representative to Angola, Haiti, and the Philippines.

And I would note parenthetically that I myself, along with a few other members, were in Aceh and applaud the work that was done during the tsunami in 2004 by CRS, and it is great to know that you were there making sure that that all happened because otherwise it would have been far worse than it actually was.

I would then like to introduce Ms. Madeline Rose, who is a policy and advocacy advisor for Mercy Corps, a global aid agency that provides assistance to those living in countries suffering from natural disaster, economic collapse, or conflict. She leads Mercy Corps' policy and advocacy portfolios on sub-Saharan African programs, including work with youth, development in fragile states, counterterrorism and humanitarian access, encountering violent extremism, and atrocity prevention.

She has also worked for the Friends Committee on National Legislation, in Congress, at the United Nations with community-based organizations in Zimbabwe, South Africa, and for the Silicon Valley tech company, NetApp.

We will then hear from Mr. Kasper Agger who is a Uganda-based field researcher for the Enough Project. We certainly have had John Prendergast here many times, who heads up Enough, a nongovernmental initiative dedicated to ending genocide and crimes against humanity. His work focuses on the Lord's Resistance Army and includes on-the-ground research in the remote areas of Uganda, South Sudan, the Democratic Republic of the Congo, and the Central African Republic, that have been most affected by the LRA crisis.

Mr. Agger's advocacy-based research aims to identify recommendations and solutions to the LRA conflict. Prior to joining the Enough Project, he worked for the Northern Uganda Peace Initiative and the U.N. Environmental Programme.

We will then hear from the Honorable Robin Renee Sanders, who is the CEO of the FEEEDS Advocacy Initiative and and owns FE3DS, LLC, both of which craft economic development and business strategies for Africa. At these organizations, she focuses on food security, education, the environment and energy, economics, development, and self-help programs, particularly for small and medium enterprises.

Prior to this, she served as the U.S. Ambassador to Nigeria and the Republic of Congo and was the U.S. Permanent Representative to ECOWAS. She served twice as Africa Director of the National Security Council at the White House. We have a very distinguished panel of knowledgeable experts, and I would like to now yield to Mr. Campbell to begin the testimony.

STATEMENT OF MR. SCOTT CAMPBELL, REGIONAL DIRECTOR FOR CENTRAL AFRICA, CATHOLIC RELIEF SERVICES

Mr. CAMPBELL. Thank you, Chairman Smith, for this opportunity to testify on behalf of Catholic Relief Services. We are very grateful to you and your leadership and the interest in the future of the Central African Republic and its people.

So I am Scott Campbell. I am the regional director for Catholic Relief Services covering the Central Africa region, and that is seven countries, the two Congos, Rwanda, Burundi, Chad, Cameroon, and Central African Republic. CRS is present in about 100 countries around the world and providing humanitarian assistance and development programming. We have been in CAR since 1999 doing programming and work very closely with our church partners in the country. Our work is mostly funded by the U.S. Government, CRS private funds, and other Caritas sister agencies.

I was recently in CAR for a 3-week period just before Christmas to mid-January, and then again for 3 weeks in March. In fact, my colleague, Ms. Rose, I met her there during the second visit. So I would like to share with you a few ideas about what has transpired there in the country and how we are prioritizing our work.

First of all, CRS is present throughout the whole breadth of the country, from the southeast covering Obo, Zinga, Rafai, Bangassou, in the LRA-affected areas. And we have a very important USAID-funded program there, working with communities affected by the Lord's Resistance Army. We are present in the capital with our partners, in the south in Lobaye Province, Mbaike, and Boda, as well as in the northwest in Bossangoa and Boda. And during my most recent trip I was in Bossangoa and saw the refugees, as you explained earlier in this testimony.

And during that visit, I was involved with the distribution of non-food items to communities that just a few weeks prior had been attacked by Seleka rebels, and this was in the area called Kuki. That whole area had been completely pillaged or burned down, and almost all of the houses, people had very little left, and of course, as you are well aware, people had very little to begin with even before the crisis. So the situation is truly desperate for tens of thousands of people.

CRS is also distributing, and will be, 7,500 households, reaching 37,500 people. We have done that already in Bossangoa, and we will do the same in the coming months in Bossangoa as well as Lobaye in the south. In those same areas, we have an initial plan to provide shelter kits for households that have been destroyed during the same month, in May, and the kits include wood for windows, doors, and tarps for roofing.

The pillaging and destruction has also rendered much of the country extremely food-insecure. This is the second consecutive planting season that has been hampered by the crisis. Seeds, tools, farm animals are scarce or non-existent in much of the region. And with the planting season upon us, CRS is distributing seeds for staple crops and farming tools for 10,000 households to respond to the critical food security situation.

Additionally, other economic activities have been disrupted, making life even more difficult. Trading and importation of goods have been hindered because Muslim traders have fled or truckers fear to enter the country because of attacks and looting.

When I was in Kuki and areas of Bossangoa, I saw heaps of cotton that had not been sold, and this is cotton that had been harvested from last year. So the much-needed cash income has not been flowing because of the crisis. And, generally, more than half the country will need some sort of humanitarian assistance as a result.

But dire as this situation is, much of what I have been describing concerns the exterior, what we see on the outside of the people who are affected. A more compelling story, however, is what is happening inside people's hearts and minds because of the problem.

It is critically important, first, to understand that this is not a religious war. No head of any faith group has led the fight against another faith group. I spoke to leaders in Bossangoa myself, including the mayor and his deputies in that city, and heard from them that they did not want to see their Muslim neighbors leaving the country.

We spoke to the youth and women of the IDP camp, Ecole Liberte, which ironically means in Liberty School when in fact it was very much like a prison. And they also expressed the desire to stay. So there is a willingness among a significant portion of the population to return to the pre-crisis reality where people lived and worked together harmoniously and in peace.

To that end, CRS has been working directly with the Inter-Religious Platform led by the Catholic Archbishop of Bangui, the President of the CAR Islamic Community, and the leader of the Evangelical Alliance. CRS has brought together faith leaders in Bangui and Bossangoa in their respective communities to participate in 2-to-3-day workshops on social cohesion and reconciliation.

This has also since included parliamentarians and other community leaders, and we are closely working with the Minister of Communications and Reconciliation of the new interim government. In fact, we will be sending her to Rwanda to see how the process worked in that country. In fact, CRS was part of that process over the past 20 years, and one of our Rwandan staff is now working in CAR to share the work he has done and learned in Rwanda there in CAR.

And this whole—the workshops we have done have been truly transformative, and I will give one example to illustrate. One of the leaders expressed how before the workshop he had every intention of buying a gun and shooting at least one person from the other faith community.

At the end of the workshop, he explained, ''I don't have those feelings anymore. I am ready for reconciliation.'' So the hate, fear, and vengeance pent up as individuals in that country, people need and feel that desire for release to just prepare themselves for reconciliation with the others in their community.

The workshops have also included Muslim faith leaders in some of the most difficult neighborhoods in Bangui where much of the fighting is evident. They were considered the hardliners. They attended and, as a result, at that time decided not to leave the country as planned. And this is just some weeks ago. If given the opportunity, the space, and the support, people in the country want to rebuild the social fabric of the society.

I saw truckloads of Muslims leaving the country during my December-January visit. Our office shares a wall with the Embassy of the Democratic Republic of the Congo, and across the street is the Ambassador to Cameroon, his residence, and they were leaving every single day. So we have seen directly people pouring out of the country.

So this is the first step. The workshops are a first step, preparing the hearts and minds of leaders and communities for peace and reconciliation, and then they can enter into a process, a dialogue, across communities. Why this is important is because it has an immediate effect, as I was saying earlier, to release people from those burdens.

But it also has the longer term effect of social cohesion to heal the wounds caused by the conflict, and which is the most effective bulwark against manipulation of the most extremist entities intent on serving their own aims in the future. It really works against the radicalization that could also be happening as these different communities move across borders.

But more funding is required to cascade that through the country. This is not something that can only be pinpointed in certain areas. It should be cascaded throughout the country. So I see that there is real hope for CAR to build back communities as before, to be productive and harmonized.

With this in mind, CRS and the USCCB make the following recommendations to the U.S. Government. First, adequately fund and support U.N. peacekeeping efforts to ensure that relief and recovery activities are tenable. Security is absolutely paramount. We need the right conditions in order to operate effectively.

Second, provide ongoing leadership and robust funding for humanitarian efforts in the CAR. The U.S. Government should also help galvanize other donors to fulfill their pledges for humanitarian assistance in the country. All efforts must support the displaced and those are hosting them to their immediate needs so that their immediate needs are met, as well as their return when conditions allow, so that they can rebuild their livelihoods, plant their farms, and support their families.

Support the voluntary return of refugees, so the country can restore its rich cultural diversity. In fact, we have plans of doing some cross-border work as well along the lines of what I described in those workshops. In fact, the workshops are actually paid by the U.S. Government. The USAID, people involved were extremely quick in releasing funding to enable us to do that in Bossangoa and then Bangui.

Also, integrate peacebuilding and conflict resolution activities to rebuild social cohesion torn apart by the recent fighting and to prevent future outbreaks of violence.

Third, affirm a commitment to CAR over the long term. We commend the appointing of a Special Representative for CAR and the U.S. Government's plan to reopen the Embassy. We further call upon the USG to develop plans to address longer term needs over the next 3 to 5 years. And this should prioritize reintegration of ex militia into economic and livelihood activities with a focus on youth. Young men need to be enrolled in reintegration programs that are practical and lead to productive job activities.

Prioritize long-term economic needs such as reconstruction of people's productive assets, keeping conflict sensitivity in mind, and recognize that elections should not be rushed. But the process fully incorporates all CAR citizens, especially those Muslims who have fled and wish to return. Any election held should be well organized, free, and fair, to end the cycle of illegitimate leaders who have neglected the needs of the Central African people.

So, Mr. Chairman and Ranking Member Bass, and the members of the subcommittee, thank you for your time, and I am——

[The prepared statement of Mr. Campbell follows:]

Testimony of
SCOTT CAMPBELL
for
CATHOLIC RELIEF SERVICES (CRS) and
THE UNITED STATES CONFERENCE OF CATHOLIC BISHOPS (USCCB)

Submitted to
The U.S. House Committee on Foreign Affairs,
Subcommittee on Africa, Global Health, Global Human Rights and International
Organizations

HEARING ON THE CRISIS IN THE CENTRAL AFRICAN REPUBLIC (CAR)
May 1, 2014

In March 2013, the Seleka rebel group, made up of mostly Muslims from Chad and Sudan, overthrew the government of President Bozizé, and as part of its short brutish rule over CAR attacked mainly Christian homes and churches and other non-Muslim communities. As the country descended into chaos, traditional self-help groups, known as Anti-Balaka, sought revenge against the Seleka and began indiscriminately killing members of the Muslim community, burning mosques and homes, causing thousands of Muslims to flee. Currently there are almost 900,000 displaced both inside and outside the country, and 2,000 reported dead.

What began as a war for power and resources with an ancillary religious dimension can now appear as a religious conflict. However, as the leaders of the Inter-Religious Platform[1] explain, this is not a religious war: "never has an Imam, a Bishop or a Pastor led the fighting or justified the killing."[2] Yet, the social fabric has been torn and the violence has affected both non-Muslim and Muslim communities. Muslim communities (15% of the population) are particularly at risk; they have been systematically under siege, with people being attacked and murdered, their homes and mosques looted and destroyed. Some of the last remaining Muslims in Bangui have just left the country, with the UN considering the forced departure of the tens of thousands of Muslims who have left as "ethnic cleansing." Non-Muslim communities also continue to be attacked by Seleka forces, particularly in the areas of the north.

African Union, French, and European Union peacekeepers are currently on the ground, yet are largely unable to contain the violence, provide adequate humanitarian access, and protect vulnerable populations. A recently passed UNSC resolution authorizes a UN Peacekeeping operation with almost 12,000 soldiers and police by September. The people of CAR, though, cannot wait till then.

Half of the country (2.7 million people) require some sort of assistance, with 1.9 million particularly at risk. In addition to immediate needs for food, shelter, protection and health care,

---

[1] The Inter-Religious Platform includes the Catholic Archbishop of Bangui, Dieudonne Nzapalainga, the leader of the Evangelical Alliance, Pastor Nicolas Geurekoyame, and the President of the CAR Islamic Community, Imam Oumar Kobine Layama. The three religious leaders are working together in CAR to promote peace among their religious groups, in efforts to quell the growing inter-religious violence.
[2] Central African Republic: Christians and Muslims Counter Ethnic Cleansing. Time Magazine. 7 April 2014.

local markets have been decimated because many of the traders and cattle herders were Muslim; local markets have run out of daily staples like sugar, flour and meat. Transport of goods into the country is a challenge and the cost of common household items, like soap, have increased 300 percent.

In my April visit to CAR, I saw the great destruction that violence had brought to the houses people lived in and the fear in people's lives, yet also saw hope that people wanted to rebuild and reconnect. In Bossangoa, where most houses had lost either their roofs or doors, people used tarps we distributed to return to their homes, while working to re-thatch their homes more permanently. I spoke with farmers eager to return to their fields to plant for the rainy season, using the seeds and tools we had distributed. They were relying on their own community structures to watch for and warn of signs of violence and danger. Continued threats of violence are on everyone's mind and we are particularly concerned about the space and ability for Muslims to return to the country.

CRS is addressing the tears in the social fabric through a project called *Mango Teré*, meaning "Come to a Consensus," which works towards reconciliation. This project expands our *Secure, Empowered and Connected Communities*, which was primarily helping communities protect themselves against LRA violence, to vulnerable areas in CAR most affected by the violence. The project works through and strengthens already existing diocesan Justice and Peace Commission (JPC) to repair the social fabric of communities through trainings led by peacebuilding experts. The project also works to strengthen community resilience against internal and external threats, assisting communities to prepare themselves for impending violence through community organization, communication and peaceful self-defense. Ultimately the goal is to enable cohesive, self-directed, and connected communities to avoid or reduce their exposure to threats associated with the presence of armed groups and ongoing conflict in areas most vulnerable to attack and ongoing interreligious/inter-communal tensions in the CAR.

Through *Mango Teré*, CRS has already seen notable glimmers of hope. As noted above, Muslims have been fleeing the country in droves. As the last Muslims were planning to leave Bangui, though, *Mango Teré* organized an event that helped the CAR government make progress in negotiations with the community. After this event, Muslims that had planned to leave decided instead to unload their trucks and stay to participate in a process of reconciliation. We see this project as an essential part of rebuilding the country, so that people can live in peace and community as they once did.

Cardinal McCarrick, a board member of CRS, a member of the USCCB Committee on International Justice and Peace, and Chair of the USCCB Ad Hoc Subcommittee for the Church in Africa, recently visited Bangui with a delegation of U.S. religious leaders, including the Imam Mohamed Magid of the Islamic Society of North America and Pastor Leith Anderson, President of the National Association of Evangelicals, in a show of solidarity with the CAR religious leaders and the communities torn apart by violence. There, they visited with communities, and as observers, signed a "Declaration for Peace" that outlines a desire for an end to violence and encourages "inter-religious dialogue."

The USCCB has worked with and supported the CAR Catholic Church to elevate the situation in the US. In July 2013, Bishop Richard E. Pates, Chair of the Committee on International Justice and Peace of the USCCB met with Bishop Nestor Desire Nongo, the Vice President of the Central African Catholic Bishops' Conference to discuss the situation in CAR and the work of the Church in the country. In a subsequent letter to the Church in CAR Bishop Pates said, "We will certainly present and advocate for your requests for increased security forces from the United Nations and the rebuilding of CAR government capacity. We will continue to urge the U.S. Government to actively support the work of the Religious Leaders Platform to rebuild social cohesion. Lastly, we will ask USAID to increase its funding for immediate emergency food and non-food items (NFI) supplies and to help civilians rebuild their institutions and their farms."

Working with Catholic Relief Services (CRS), the USCCB organized two visits by Bishop Nestor Desire Nongo Aziagbia from the Diocese of Bossangoa and Vice President of the Central African Catholic Bishops' Conference. During the first visit in September 2013, Bishop Nongo held meetings with State Department and Congressional leaders, and returned in November to testify before the House Subcommittee on Africa, Global Health, Global Human Rights and International Organizations. In March 2014 the USCCB, CRS and other NGOs sponsored a Washington visit of the Inter-Religious Leaders' Platform, consisting of the Catholic Archbishop of Bangui, Dieudonne Nzapalainga, the leader of the Evangelical Alliance, Pastor Nicolas Geurekoyame, and the President of the CAR Islamic Community, Imam Oumar Kobine Layama. The delegation held meetings with State Department, the National Security Council, the White House's Office on Faith-based and Partnership Initiatives and Congress. In July this year Bishop Pates, Chair of the U.S. bishops' Committee on International Justice and Peace, will travel to Bangui for a solidarity visit.

CRS, founded by the U.S. bishops in 1943 as the official relief and development agency of the Catholic community in our nation, has been working in Central African Republic since 2007. CRS works closely with its partners—the Catholic Church and local Caritas to assist those in need.

Understanding the state of the country, and recognizing that the people of CAR do not just need immediate assistance, but will need long-term support, CRS has committed private funding and assistance to CAR over the next five years. With this and public donor support, we will focus on three areas: 1) Immediate Relief through the provision of shelter, camp management, food and other household items; 2) Recovery activities through the provision of transitional shelter, access to livelihoods inputs (seeds and tools), cash for work, non-agricultural livelihoods and market based support, promotion of savings and lending; and 3) Community Protection/Social Cohesion, including community risk mapping and planning, establishing early warning and referral systems, training of community leaders in peace building/conflict resolution, formation and training of community cohesion committees and support for trauma healing.

With this in mind, CRS and the USCCB make the following recommendations to the U.S. Government:

1. **Adequately fund and support UN peacekeeping efforts to ensure that relief and recovery activities are tenable. The USG must ensure that the peacekeeping force:**

- Prioritizes the protection of civilians, especially women and children, led by communities as they return to their homes, and works to ensure that Muslim refugee communities are safe to return from neighboring countries.
- Has strong communications and command and control structures that clearly lay out how the PKO will engage existing troops (AU, French and EU) on the ground.
- Has sufficient high-quality, well-trained troops from neutral countries who do not act with ulterior motives.
- Works to ensure the country remains one, and that surrounding countries do not undermine the unity of the country.

2. **Provide ongoing leadership and robust funding for humanitarian efforts in CAR. The USG should also help galvanize other donors to fulfill their pledges for humanitarian assistance in CAR. All efforts must:**
   - Support the displaced and those who are hosting them so their immediate needs are met, as well as their return when conditions allow so that they can rebuild their livelihoods, plant their farms, and support their families.
   - Support the voluntary return of refugees so the country can restore it rich cultural diversity. This will depend on the security of the country, but should allow for safe passage and secure existence for Muslim populations who desire to return.
   - Develop a regional plan for refugees who have fled to neighboring countries that are already heavily burdened with their own populations' needs.
   - Integrate peacebuilding and conflict resolution activities to rebuild social cohesion torn apart by the recent fighting and to prevent future outbreaks of violence.
   - Ensure conflict sensitive approaches to humanitarian assistance. This requires a full understanding of the conflict and risks involved with providing certain types of assistance so that it does not de facto support one group over another. The USG should also consider support for increasing the capacity of the humanitarian community to ensure assistance does no harm.

3. **Affirm a commitment to CAR over the long term. We commend the appointment of a Special Representative for CAR, and the U.S. Government's plans to re-open the Embassy. We further call upon the USG to develop plans to address longer term needs (3-5 years) that:**
   - Addresses the needs of the CAR government to build capacity to provide government services and exercise functional control over the country. One urgent priority is the rebuilding of the local police and security structures which need training and accompaniment. Without security and stabilization, the culture of impunity will continue, and the cycle of violence will no doubt continue.
   - Prioritizes full USG presence in country so that it can play a leadership role and work with other governments to ensure a robust response and recovery, as well as longer term development plans.
   - Prioritizes reintegration of ex-militia into economic and livelihood activities with a focus on youth. Young men need to be enrolled in reintegration programs that are practical and lead to productive job activities;
   - Prioritizes longer-term economic needs such as reconstruction of people's productive assets, keeping conflict sensitivity in mind;

- Recognizes that elections should not be rushed, but the process fully incorporates all CAR citizens, especially those Muslims who have fled and wish to return. Any election held should be well-organized, free and fair to end the cycle of illegitimate leaders who have neglected the needs of the Central African people.

Mr. SMITH. No. Thank you very much for your solid recommendations. Thank you for the good work that Cardinal McCarrick and so many others have done. His most recent visit I think was galvanizing and underscored the point you made so strongly, and that is that this is not about leaders of religious faiths conducting either a jihad or any kind of a religious war, but people are exploiting extremism in order to kill and to rape and to maim. So thank you for bringing that strongly forward.

I would like to now recognize Ms. Rose.

STATEMENT OF MS. MADELINE ROSE, POLICY & ADVOCACY ADVISOR, MERCY CORPS

Ms. ROSE. Thank you, Chairman. And I would like to submit my full written testimony for the record.

Mr. SMITH. Without objection, so ordered.

Ms. ROSE. Thank you. Chairman Smith, Ranking Member Bass, and members of the subcommittee, thank you for inviting me to testify on behalf of Mercy Corps today, and for your leadership in mobilizing what has become a robust and generous U.S. Government response to the crisis in the Central African Republic.

My name is Madeline Rose, and I am a policy advisor for Mercy Corps, a global humanitarian agency working in over 40 crisis-affected countries in the world. Mercy Corps has worked in CAR since 2007, managing programs ranging from emergency response and conflict mitigation to youth empowerment and economic development.

If there is one message that I hope you take from this testimony, it is that right now is the moment to secure long-term support for CAR's recovery. The window for influence is closing, and we have to make smart investments now.

In March, I traveled to Bouar to visit Mercy Corps' conflict mitigation and protection programs. The most heartbreaking meeting of my trip was the one I expected to be easiest. I met a judge with whom we have worked on access to justice programs for survivors of gender-based violence. I asked what challenges he was facing and how the international community could be helpful.

His response was simple. He asked for replacement pencils and papers, which had been looted during the crisis, so that he could get back to work processing rape cases. Pencils. Conflict waged all around us. Across the street I could see civilians preparing convoys to flee to Cameroon, yet his primary request was for a pencil to go back to work and restore a semblance of justice to his community.

I told this story because it underscores the complexity of an overlooked element of the CAR crisis right now. We are dealing with a multi-faceted conflict and a humanitarian catastrophe in one of the poorest and most underdeveloped countries in the world. This means that every humanitarian activity will be more expensive, capacity-building will fundamentally take longer, and political and economic recovery will require long-term sustained engagement.

Three weeks after this subcommittee's November 19 hearing on the crisis, anti-balaka attacked CAR's capital, Bangui, triggering a brutal cycle of retaliation killings between Christians and Muslims that continues to this day. As other witnesses have testified here today, the cycle of retaliatory violence has spiraled so far out of control that it has deteriorated into ethno-religious cleansing.

Ever more alarmingly, Mercy Corps sees many of the same trends emerging in CAR today that we have seen before in the DRC, the Sudans, and other contexts that become entrenched in protracted violence. This includes criminality, banditry, sexual abuses, and other crimes being committed with impunity across the country, massive and protracted displacement and protection crises developing in ungoverned and difficult-to-access or militia-controlled territories, citizens growing impatient with the absence of services from the transitional government, losing faith in the prospects of legitimate civilian rule, armed actors actively targeting and recruiting disaffected youth, and, most alarmingly, popular support for de facto ethno-religious partition of the country that would divide the country between north and south along major natural resource belts.

If we fail to address CAR's crisis quickly and correctly, Mercy Corps is concerned that the situation could metastasize into a new decades-long conflict transcending the Sahel to South Sudan. While the current situation is horrific, it is not hopeless. There are promising examples of community-based protection and peacebuilding all across the country. Humanitarian development and peacebuilding organizations have the commitment and absorptive capacity to scale up operations if additional funding is made available.

Mercy Corps currently sees five priorities, each of which must be met and addressed simultaneously. The first, as my colleague said, is to restore security and reinforce civilian protection. Mercy Corps concurs fully with the Catholic Relief Services' request for full peacekeeping funding, and we would also like to add two quick additions. The first, that Congress consult regularly with the interagency to ensure maximum U.S. support to MISCA in the interim, and also to see what creative non-financial diplomatic tools we might be able to leverage that haven't been pulled out of the toolbox just yet.

And then, secondly, just to underscore my colleague's comments about not rushing toward elections, we strongly oppose efforts to accelerate elections toward a February 2015 deadline if those processes would exacerbate the risk of violence against civilians or undermine the legitimate prospects for peace.

Secondly, we ask for an increase in support for peacebuilding and reconciliation initiatives. The deployment of military and police alone will not ensure peace and security in CAR, as you well know. As CAR's senior-most religious leaders stated on their visit to Washington, DC, we must disarm the hearts and minds of Central Africans.

Third, we ask for you to fulfill urgent humanitarian needs. The degree of human suffering is staggering, as you well know, yet the 2014 global humanitarian appeal is only 28 percent funded. The first priority for Congress should be protecting appropriations funding for the International Disaster Assistance and Migration and Refugee Assistance Accounts.

Unfortunately, the administration's FY2015 budget request to Congress cuts IDA by 28 percent and MRA by 33 percent. If enacted, international responders will have a very difficult time addressing the humanitarian needs.

Fourth, target interventions toward the protection and empowerment of women and girls. From January to March of this year, over 90 percent of the rape cases we have seen in our centers have been gang rapes committed by armed actors. This is a very significant increase in rape cases that Mercy Corps has seen in the Central African Republic. In addition, women have been marginalized across all aspects of the response and risking marginalized and reconciliation and recovery processes as well.

Fifth, secure commitments now for transition. To date, the U.S. has not committed funds or communicated its strategic intentions in CAR beyond December 2014. This sends mixed signals to Central Africans, partners, and the international community about U.S. intentions to engage in the medium to long term. Efforts to reopen the U.S. Embassy in Bangui should be prioritized and expedited, and Congress could also be very helpful in accelerating the engagement of international financial institutions in CAR.

Twenty years after the Rwandan genocide and subsequent crisis in GRC, as you so eloquently stated in your opening remarks, Mr. Chairman, the U.S. has stated that the prevention of mass atrocities constitutes a core moral and national security priority. If the U.S. takes its commitments to preventing mass atrocities seriously, now is the moment to secure long-term support for CAR's recovery. Atrocities prevention cannot be understood simply as mobilizing resources in the face of imminent or already-ongoing atrocities against civilians. It must be seen as investing in infrastructure to mitigate them long before they start.

There is a long road ahead for recovery in CAR, but recovery is possible and critical. Thank you again for the opportunity to testify and for your continued support to the people of the Central African Republic. I look forward to any questions.

[The prepared statement of Ms. Rose follows:]

 MercyCorps

mercycorps.org

Testimony of Madeline Rose
Policy & Advocacy Advisor, Mercy Corps

Hearing on the Crisis in the Central African Republic

Submitted to the House Foreign Affairs Subcommittee on Africa, Global Health, Global Human Rights,
and International Organizations

01 May 2014

Chairman Smith, Ranking Member Bass, and Members of the Committee, thank you for the invitation to
testify on behalf of Mercy Corps today, and for your leadership in mobilizing what has become a robust
U.S. government response to the horrific and complex crisis in the Central African Republic (CAR).

My name is Madeline Rose and I am a Policy Advisor for Mercy Corps, a global humanitarian agency
working in over 40 conflict or crisis affected countries in the world. Mercy Corps has worked in CAR
since 2007. We have five offices, in Bangui, Bouar, Bangassou, Bambari and Rafai, managing programs
ranging from emergency response and conflict mitigation, to youth empowerment and agriculture and
economic development. We are proud partners of the U.S. government in CAR and globally.

If there is one message that I hope you take from this testimony, it is that resolving the current crisis in
CAR will require long term commitments from the U.S. and international community. Immediate
security and humanitarian assistance is urgent and needed, but will prove futile if not simultaneously
reinforced by efforts to address the root causes of the country's chronic insecurity.

A VIEW FROM BOUAR

In March, I traveled to Bouar – one of the most economically and militarily strategic towns in CAR given
its proximity to the Cameroonian border – to visit Mercy Corps' conflict mitigation and protection
programs. The most heartbreaking meeting of my trip was one I expected to be easiest.

Mercy Corps collaborates with our local partner, the Central African Women's Lawyers Association, to
provide holistic services to survivors of gender-based violence (GBV) in Bouar, which includes psycho-
social counseling, community-based mediation, and paralegal assistance. Prior to this current conflict,
the program included an "access to justice" element, which supported survivors of GBV seek judicial
recourse for abuses committed against them, while helping to build judicial and governance capacities.
During this most recent conflict, however, CAR's judicial systems have grounded to a halt.

I met a judge with whom we've partnered, and asked what challenges he faced and how the
international community could be helpful. His response was simple: he asked for replacement pencils
and paper, resources that had been looted and destroyed during the conflict, so that he could get back
to work documenting and processing rape cases. Pencils. Conflict waged all around us. Across the street,

civilians prepared convoys to flee to Cameroon. Yet his primary request was for a pencil to go back to work and restore a semblance of justice in his community.

I tell this story because it underscores an underemphasized element of the CAR crisis: we are dealing with an extraordinarily multifaceted conflict and a humanitarian catastrophe in one of the poorest and most underdeveloped countries in the world. This means that every humanitarian activity will be more expensive; capacity building will take longer; and political and economic recovery will require long term, sustained engagement.

ROOTS OF THE CRISIS

The current crisis in CAR is the result of a long historical process. Since its independence in 1960, CAR has been plagued by poor governance, trapping the country in a cycle of conflict and underdevelopment. Political elites and rapacious neighbors have exploited the country's lawlessness and porous borders for decades, extracting the country's natural resources for personal enrichment while investing little in the future of the Central African people. A legacy of predatory state institutions and a culture of corruption and cronyism have undermined leaders' accountability to their citizens.

CAR is also chronically poor, with little natural resource wealth, and until recently, utterly neglected by the international community. Prior to this current wave of violence, close to two-thirds of the population lived on less than $1.25 per day and the country ranked 181st on UNDP's Human Development Index of 187 countries. In a March 2012 situation report – one year before the ex-Séléka coup ousted former President Bozize – Operations Director of the United Nations Office for the Coordination of Humanitarian Affairs (OCHA), John Ging, stated that, "CAR continues to face one of the world's worst humanitarian funding shortfalls." Further, there has been almost no concerted development action in CAR since the early 1990s beyond short-term responses to immediate, recurrent, emergencies.

The current armed conflict between the ex-Séléka rebel alliance and Anti-Balaka militia has exacerbated CAR's challenges in significant ways. Previously weak and unorganized armed groups are now emboldened. Violent sectarian divisions between civilians have been fomented, and a wave of criminality and banditry has surged across the country. The country's already weak physical infrastructure has been obliterated, and one-fifth of CAR's entire population has been displaced by violence. The government is completely broke, unable to control the violence that has been unleashed. In a country where the civil service is one of the few avenues to middle class employment, civil servants have received only one month of their salaries since July 2013.

CONFLICT TRENDS OF PARTICULAR CONCERN

Three weeks after this Committee's Nov. 19th hearing on this crisis, Anti-Balaka attacked CAR's capital, Bangui, triggering a brutal cycle of retaliation killings between Muslim and Christians that continues to this day. There are five trends of particular concern we see at this time.

1. **The cycle of retaliatory violence has escalated into ethno-religious cleansing.** Since the December 5th attack on Bangui, ex-Séléka began to retreat north while Anti-Balaka grew in number and ferocity, exacerbating prevailing lawlessness across the country. Both armed groups, as well as other opportunistic armed actors, manipulated this security vacuum, playing on frustrations of oppressive rule

by both armed groups and deep seated mistrust and resentment between communities, to divide Central Africans along socio-economic and religious lines.

Muslims have since come under deliberate and systematic attack by Anti-Balaka militias and mobs of ordinary civilians. Meanwhile, ex-Séléka and Muslim civilians continue to commit horrific abuses and killings against Christian civilians. Despite the presence of African Union and French peacekeepers, ordinary citizens continue to engage in opportunistic violence or be instrumentalized—in particular disaffected youth—by the militia groups.

The UN Office for the Coordination of Humanitarian Affairs (OCHA) estimates that eighty-five percent of CAR's Muslim population has been forced to flee, and those remaining are at high risk of attack. They determined that the violence constitutes "massive ethno-religious cleansing," and issued a decision to assist Muslim population movements as necessary in order to save lives. This is a rare and high risk decision for the agency, underscoring the severity of the situation.

2. Insecurity, criminality and lawlessness persist across the country. Despite the presence of peacekeepers, a transitional government and revival of some economic activity, insecurity is surging. Routine killings, lootings, robberies, sexual abuses and other crimes are committed daily with impunity across the country, including in Bangui. Right now, we need to be looking forward to anticipate and prevent the next crises – which will likely be in Boda and Bambari on major axes outside of Bangui, around the mines in Bria, Ndele and the north, and among refugees and host communities across the country in the region – but current response structures will fail to prevent future crises so long as already strained peacekeeping resources fail to quell widespread lawlessness.

3. Citizens are growing impatient with the transitional government, losing faith in the prospects of legitimate civilian rule. Civil servants have not been paid, government buildings have been destroyed, and the justice system is in disarray. Civilians want to see the transitional government provide basic services, and perpetrators of crimes and abuses held accountable under law. Each day the conflict continues, youth and vulnerable populations become more hopeless about the future of their country.

4. A massive and protracted displacement crisis is developing in ungoverned and difficult to access regions. According to an April OCHA situation report, there are 325,179 refugees from CAR in neighboring countries and roughly 700,000 internally displaced. This means hundreds of thousands of Central Africans now live in ungoverned or militia-controlled regions. Ex-Séléka control the north and northeastern regions, while Anti-Balaka control most of the South and Southeast. Humanitarian actors are sparsely populated in CAR, especially in the north, and are increasingly struggling to access civilians in militia-controlled territories. Roads are rare in rural CAR, and with the onset of rainy season, many will be impassable for months.

Sunday's attack by ex-Séléka on a clearly marked Medecins Sans Frontieres (MSF) hospital in Boguila that killed 15 local chiefs and 3 MSF national staff tragically highlights this challenge. MSF was the only humanitarian organization in Boguila, a town on the main road from Bangui to Chad, and is now in the difficult position of re-assessing the security risks of delivery.

5. Popular support for ethno-religious partition of the country is increasing. On its current trajectory, partition would divide the country along religious lines, into North/South, split along major natural resource belts and pastoralist divides. Partition would be disastrous for CAR's economy and social fabric; it would also legitimize ethnic cleansing and make reconciliation efforts more challenging.

RISK OF FURTHER REGIONALIZATION

If we fail to address CAR's crisis quickly and correctly, Mercy Corps is concerned that the situation could metastasize into a new decades-long conflict transcending the corridor from the Sahel to South Sudan – curtailing development and threatening regional stability. Displacement sites in the above-described ungoverned areas could become breeding grounds for radicalization and recruitment of disaffected youth into violence.

Between CAR and the neighboring crisis in South Sudan, two million people are newly displaced across the region, putting further pressure on already stretched local, national and international response resources. This is the precise lawlessness that attracts regional opportunists, such as wildlife poachers from DRC and Sudan, and the Lord's Resistance Army, which has moved deeper into northwest CAR in the last six months and started attacking more civilians than they have in years.

PRIORITIES FOR INTERNATIONAL RESPONSE

While the current situation is horrific, it is not hopeless. There are promising examples of community based protection and peacebuilding across the country, including in Bambari where local Imams and Priests have negotiated peaceful co-habitation for their communities, and in Bouar where integrated Muslim and Christian schools have re-opened. Humanitarian, development and peacebuilding organizations have the commitment and absorptive capacity necessary to scale up their operations if additional funding is made available.

However, support must increase. There is a real danger that international attention will wane now that the UN peacekeeping mission, MINUSCA, has been authorized, and in a few years we will see a Central African state that is every bit as fragile, underdeveloped, and incapable of preventing a crisis like the one we are discussing here today. We see five priorities, each of which must be met and addressed simultaneously.

1. Restore security and reinforce civilian protection immediately. MISCA and Sangaris peacekeeping forces have not been able to restore security. Even with the anticipated EU reinforcements, the enormity of the challenges will outstrip capacities. The most urgent priorities include:
- generating impartial peacekeepers to replace the 850 Chadian peacekeepers withdrawn;
- increasing the number and capacity of police and civilian units within MISCA;
- immediately instituting a peacekeeper vetting system using the UN Human Rights Due Diligence Policy and ensuring trainings in international humanitarian law, do no harm, and proactive civilian peacekeeping for all incoming peacekeepers, and
- keeping the humanitarian response independent of the peacekeeping operation as MISCA transitions into MINUSCA to ensure that all communities can be reached with impartial assistance.

Ensuring that a broad, inclusive national dialogue focused on the key issues of the future of the country takes place before elections is also a key priority. Among the most fundamental underpinnings of CAR's chronic insecurity is the perception amongst elites and civilians alike that politics is a zero sum, winner-takes-all process. We strongly oppose efforts to accelerate elections towards February 2015 if such process would exacerbate risks of violence against civilians or undermine legitimate peace prospects. It is critical, as noted in UNSCR Res 2149 authorizing MINUSCA, displaced persons and refugees must be registered and included in this process, lest they become further disenfranchised.

Importantly for Congress, this also means authorizing funds to cover U.S. contributions to the recently authorized UN Peacekeeping Mission in the CAR, MINUSCA. In this light, we urge Congress to fully fund the President's FY2015 Peacekeeping requests, including the Peacekeeping Response Mechanism. Even if the PKRM is not used in CAR, rapid response funding structures are necessary in the absence of supplemental appropriations bills, as we've now seen with Mali and the CAR.

2. Support peacebuilding and reconciliation initiatives. The deployment of military and police alone will not suffice to ensure peace and security. As CAR's senior most religious leaders, Imam Omar Kobine Layama, Archbishop Dieudonné Nzapalainga, and Reverend Nicolas Guérékoyame-Gbangou stated on their visit to Washington DC, we "must disarm hearts and minds simultaneously as we take weapons away." There are many new initiatives that warrant investment, and a need for global donors – including the U.S. – to ensure coordination so as to not overwhelm local capacity.

Initiatives should integrate conflict mitigation and tolerance building – focused on youth, religious communities, women – assets protection for displaced populations, livelihoods, and media. In the west, for example, Mercy Corps is partnering with the Bouar Inter-Religious Platform to help restore social cohesion by facilitating inclusive, community-led processes to address grievances and rebuild intercommunal tolerance and increase economic cooperation across lines of division and. The western region of the country holds the best prospects for reconciliation so efforts there should be protected and scaled up as an example for national recovery.

3. Fulfill urgent humanitarian needs. The degree of human suffering is staggering. 2014 Global Humanitarian appeal is only 28% funded. In recent weeks, the International Committee for the Red Cross and UNHAS have cancelled flights due to lack of fuel. Traveling by road is impossible to many parts of the country, such as Bambari and the southeast, due to fighting in the Grimari area. Cancelling flights makes these destinations completely unreachable.

The first priority for Congress should be protecting appropriations funding for the International Disaster Assistance (IDA) and Migration and Refugee Assistance (MRA) Accounts to ensure humanitarian needs can be meet throughout FY 2014 and into FY 2015. Unfortunately, the Administration's FY2015 budget request to Congress cuts IDA, the account that deals with displaced persons, by 28% from FY14 levels, and MRA, the account that deals with refugees, by 33%. The U.S. could also help by encouraging other donors to fulfill their Brussels pledges.

4. Target interventions towards the protection and empowerment of women and girls. From January-March, 70% of the cases we have received in our listening center in Bangui have been for rape. Of these cases, over 90% of these rapes have been gang rapes committed by armed actors. This is a massive increase in rape trends compared to any caseloads Mercy Corps has ever received in CAR. Worse, the migratory season is approaching, during which Central African women and families are often left at home alone as men search for employment elsewhere in the country. But this year women and girls will face abandonment in a much higher risk security context. Beyond gender-based violence, women have been marginalized across many aspects of the response and risk being marginalized in reconciliation and recovery platforms as well.

5. Secure commitments now for staebuilding, transition and long term development. There are four major issues to address for CAR's transition: disarmament, demobilization and reintegration of combatants, security and judiciary sector reform, elections and economic recovery. These are complex issues that have failed repeatedly in CAR's history, and will require strategic thinking and long-term resources to be done well. Moreover, while these issues may seem distant, longer term development and diplomatic investments can help prevent violence *today* by giving youth and key community influencers hope, rebuilding economic ties and kick-starting local economies, and building platforms for meaningful civic engagement.

To date, the U.S. has not committed funding to the crisis beyond December 2014. This sends mixed signals to Central Africans, partners and the international community about U.S. intentions to engage in the medium-to-long term. In Mercy Corps' experience implementing over 100 conflict programs around the world, one of the clearest lessons we have learned is to build as much flexibility as possible into program design. This is especially true in CAR, where the context remains extremely fluid. Flexible, multi-year assistance is the best way to ensure a conflict-sensitive transition from relief to development.

Immediately, CAR's transitional government needs an immediate support package to pay civil servant salaries, restore basic state functions, and begin this planning process. Efforts to re-open the U.S. Embassy in Bangui should also be prioritized, and Congress should help accelerate international financial institution (IFI) engagement in CAR.

CONCLUSION

As this Subcommittee knows, 2014 marks the 20-year anniversaries of both the 100-day Rwandan genocide and the subsequent crisis in DRC that has taken 5.4 million lives and continues to this day. Consecutive U.S. administrations have expressed frustration about our collective inability to prevent such crises, and in 2010, the U.S. affirmed for the first time that the prevention of mass atrocities and genocide constitutes a core moral and national security priority to the U.S.

Within this context, the U.S. response to CAR's crisis marks an important shift in U.S. foreign policy: the alignment of political will, policy, rapid funding structures, and enhanced information-sharing and decision-making processes for the prevention of mass atrocities has indeed changed how the U.S. engages in potential atrocity situations. However, the response was too late. Despite many warning signs of the crisis, the U.S. failed to mobilize a response until mass violence was already underway.

If the U.S. takes its commitment to preventing mass atrocities seriously, now is the moment to secure long term resources to support CAR's recovery. Mass atrocities prevention should not be understood only as mobilizing resources in the face of imminent or already ongoing atrocities, but rather, as investing in the infrastructure to mitigate them before they start.

There is a long road ahead for recovery in CAR, but recovery is possible and critical.

Thank you again for the opportunity to testify and for your continued support to the people of the Central African Republic. I look forward to answering any questions.

51

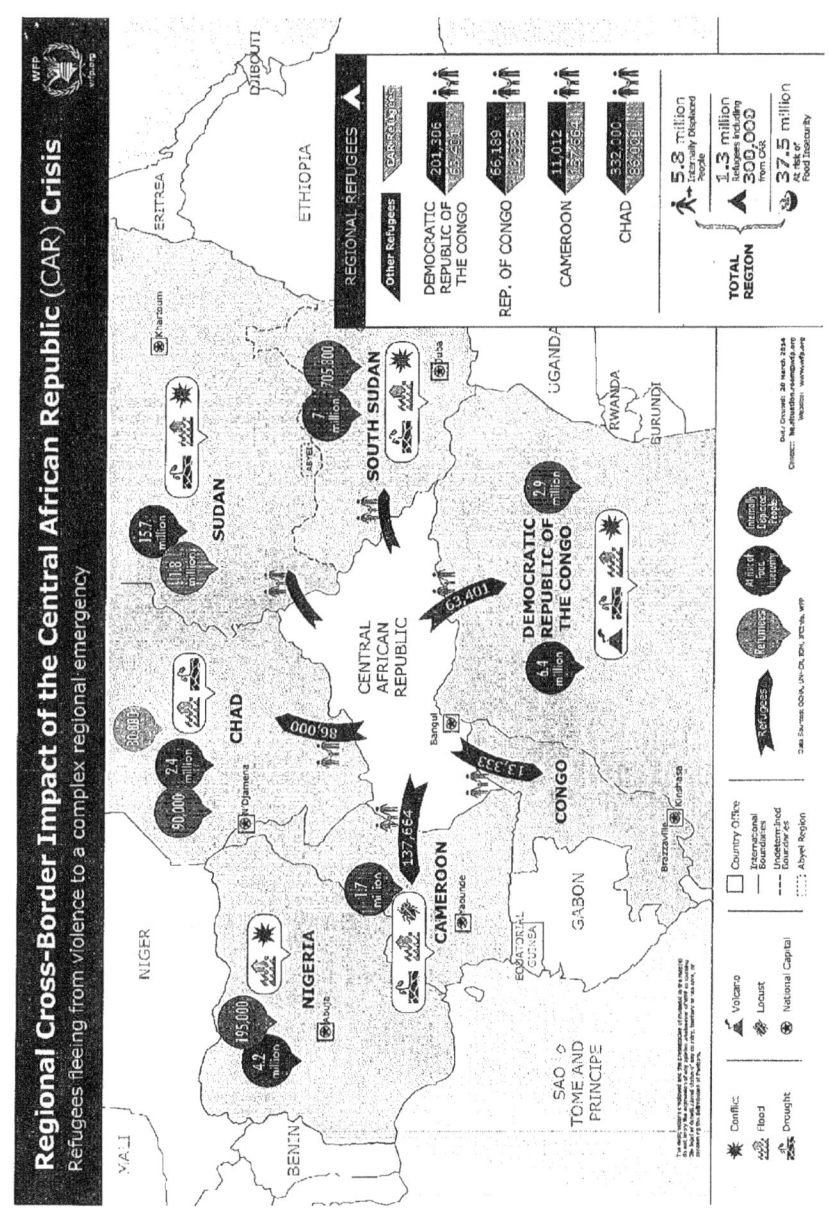

Regional Cross-Border Impact of the Central African Republic (CAR) Crisis
Refugees fleeing from violence to a complex regional emergency

Mr. SMITH. Thank you very, very much for your testimony and your work.

Mr. Agger.

STATEMENT OF MR. KASPER AGGER, FIELD RESEARCHER, ENOUGH PROJECT

Mr. AGGER. Chairman Smith, Ranking Member Bass, members of the subcommittee, thank you very much for this opportunity to testify at this critical moment for the Central African Republic.

I have been working as a field researcher with the Enough Project and traveled to the country over the past 2 years, last time in February, where I spent 3 weeks in the capital, Bangui, looking at the drivers of the violence, the armed actors, and the role of natural resources, and the prospects for sustainable peace.

I interviewed Seleka fighters, anti-balaka fighters, members of the transitional government, aid workers, and local journalists. I also talked with the business sector, with diamond traders, and people with firsthand knowledge of ivory poaching in the country. I also went to the IDP camps and met many of the displaced people.

The people I interviewed told me that what has been described as religious conflict goes much deeper. The crisis stems from a lack of leadership and exclusion of the people from the decisionmaking process. What unites groups of fighters is not so much religion but social, economic, and political grievances from decades of marginalization. Many combatants are motivated by the promises of economic gains rather than religion.

Central African fighters and the allies are part of a broader regional and international conflict system in which outside countries and armed groups compete for state-controlled natural resources and a general influence for resources in Central Africa. I also learned from my interviews that diamonds and elephant ivory are funding the Seleka, the notorious Janjaweed militia from Sudan, including the anti-balaka, who have all controlled diamond-rich areas and sell diamonds and ivory to fund their activities.

Natural resources have also attracted the Governments of Chad, Sudan, South Africa, China, and France. Interventions by these governments have influenced security dynamics in the country. The interest of Chad and Sudan especially has contributed to the conflict. Mercenary fighters from each of these countries were part of the Seleka movement and committed horrible atrocities and looted.

The international community as a whole can take a few critical steps, but we must act as quickly as possible. First, deploy mediators to facilitate a bottom-up peace and reconciliation process. We must support efforts to rebuild the state institutions that have come to a virtual standstill.

We must investigate illicit diamond and ivory trading in the region and cut off funding sources for the armed groups. We must hold accountable those who commit atrocities and engage in economic and criminal activity. Sustained U.S. diplomatic engagement in the region that recognizes and addresses the interest of the many actors who are involved, and that targets the illicit sources of financing for violent actors, can directly contribute to sustainable peace.

If the U.S. Government pursues low-cost diplomatic initiatives now that boost international efforts, we could prevent mass atrocities in the long run. Americans have provided vital financial and diplomatic support for the international peacemaking efforts and to MISCA. The appointment of Ambassador Symington as U.S. Special Representative for CAR will add momentum to these efforts.

As the U.S. charts the future of its critical engagement, I urge Congress and the administration to not only target the most acute, immediate needs in the country, but also to pursue sustained engagement that addresses the root causes of the conflict. Otherwise, I fear that we will not be able to bring a sustainable peace to the country, which has experienced more than five military coups since independence in 1960.

First, the U.S. should continue to support MISCA and provide strong support for the U.N. peacekeeping mission. Further, it should encourage the U.N. to promote an inclusive bottom-up peace and reconciliation process in the country, the decentralized nature of the conflict, the profusion of different actors, and the lack of a central command for many of the armed groups all mean that the nation requires a bottom-up peace approach that addresses the armed groups through local negotiations and local dialogues and reconciliation processes.

I would also like to reinforce that reconciliation should be broad-based and not only between religious groups. Many people take up arms in pursuit of economic interests, so we need to include civil society, women leaders, youth groups, a broad range of actors, in the reconciliation process.

Second, the U.S. should work with international partners to cut off sources of financing to violent groups. The United States and China, as current chair of the Kimberley Process, should press for the Kimberley Process to lead review missions to the United Arab Emirates, Belgium, and India to investigate the smuggling of conflict diamonds from the country. These efforts could identify individuals and companies against whom the United States and the U.N. could issue target sanctions.

Third, the U.S. should adopt a regional approach to diplomatic engagement. There is an urgent need to recognize the motivating interest of those who are drawn to the natural resources and exploit fragile state institutions in the search for profits. The tri-border region between the Central African Republic, Chad, and Sudan is a largely lawless area where rebel groups operate relatively freely. The U.S. should work with international partners to develop a common policy for the region.

America must continue to lead with and alongside international partners to address violence in the country. The country's most precious resources, its people, deserve nothing less.

Thank you very much. I will be happy to take any questions you might have.

[The prepared statement of Mr. Agger follows:]

1332 K Street NW, 14th Floor, Washington, DC 20005
Phone: 202.682.1611 ● Fax: 202.682.6140 ● www.enoughproject.org
A PROJECT OF THE CENTER FOR AMERICAN PROGRESS

Testimony of Kasper Agger
Field Researcher, Enough Project
U.S. House of Representatives Committee on Foreign Affairs, Subcommittee on Africa,
Global Health, Global Human Rights and International Organizations
Hearing on "The Central African Republic: From "Pre-genocide" to Genocide?"
May 1, 2014

Introduction

Thank you very much for the opportunity to testify, Chairman Smith and Ranking Member Bass, at this crucial moment for the Central African Republic.

I traveled to the Central African Republic in February 2014 and spent three weeks in Bangui analyzing the interests, the activities, and the funding sources of armed groups and governments that have become involved in CAR. During my stay, I interviewed Séléka fighters, Anti-Balaka fighters, and Central African government officials. I visited a barracks where about a thousand Séléka fighters were waiting for disarmament to begin. I spoke with many people about the revenues and funding sources for the Séléka and other armed groups in CAR. I began to identify the ties between these armed actors and elephant poaching and the illicit diamond trade.

Combatants, politicians, businessmen, and diplomats were all giving me the same reasons for the crisis in their country. They said it is lack of leadership and exclusion of citizens from the decision-making process that is fueling the violence. I also came to realize from the interviews that natural resources and the often overlooked regional interests of CAR's neighbors are major causes of the conflict.

The U.S. government is starting to contribute to the solution to the CAR crisis, but a low-cost initiative to boost this effort would have a major impact in preventing the next round of mass atrocities. The United States has responded to developments and advocacy efforts with financial and diplomatic support. The recent appointment of Ambassador Symington as U.S. Special Representative for CAR will add momentum to these diplomatic efforts.

As the U.S. crafts the future of its critical engagement in CAR, I urge Congress and the Administration to not only target the acute, immediate needs created by the conflict but also pursue sustained U.S. engagement that addresses the core underlying drivers of conflict that could incite continuing cycles of violence. This can be done at a low cost with diplomatic efforts within CAR and outside to pressure CAR's neighbors and the financiers of violence. The U.S. should work with the U.N. to encourage an inclusive, bottom-up peace and reconciliation process. The U.S. should work with international partners to cut off sources of financing to actors who perpetrate violence. And the U.S. should adopt a regional approach to diplomatic engagement. A wide range of armed actors and governments have a history of involvement in CAR's affairs. Addressing the economic and security interests that motivate these actors is vitally important to building a successful international approach.

The need for an inclusive peace process

CAR has been on a downward development spiral since its independence in 1960 from France. It has experienced five military coups and ranks 180 out of 186 countries on the U.N. Human Development Index. Previous leaders of CAR, including former President François Bozizé, monopolized power and turned the country into a profitable venture for family and personal friends, while the population suffered. CAR has never addressed its troubled past, and former leaders enjoy impunity. In the past 12 months, however, CAR has experienced unprecedented levels of violence and mass killings of thousands of civilians. Roughly one million people, a quarter of the population, have been displaced. The Central African state has come close to a complete standstill and lacks a functioning army, police force, and justice system. When I visited, I saw that the political process has stalled, and the transitional government has very little leverage over those who carry arms and kill.

The decentralized nature of the conflict in CAR, the profusion of different actors, and the lack of a central command for many armed groups, all mean that the nation requires a bottom-up peace approach that addresses armed groups through local negotiations. Central Africans cannot wait for a ceasefire; they need a political reconciliation process to begin immediately at the local level. The U.S. can, through the leadership of Special Representative Symington, work alongside a diverse group of CAR leaders and the international community to begin building such a process immediately. Top-down negotiations among leaders of armed factions and political elites in Bangui will not break the political deadlock and end the violence—because those leaders cannot control the myriad armed groups. National and local-level dialogues must instead prominently feature the voices of civil society actors, including women, traditional leaders, religious figures, and youth.

Drivers of violence: Diamonds and poaching

What appears on the surface as religious violence between Muslim Séléka rebels and Christian Anti-Balaka militias actually goes much deeper. In speaking with many of these combatants, I found that both Séléka and Anti-Balaka fighters are actually united less by religion than by socio-economic and political grievances. These groups have been marginalized for decades by political leaders. Many are motivated by revenge for past grievances, the need for self-defense, and the promise of economic gains. These Central African fighters and their allies are part of a broader regional and international conflict system in which outside countries and armed groups pursue state control, natural resources, economic gains, and influence in Central Africa. Sustained regional U.S. diplomatic engagement that recognizes and addresses the interests of these many actors, and that targets the illicit sources of financing for violent actors, can directly contribute to sustainable peace in the Central African Republic.

My research on the economic drivers of conflict in the Central African Republic, published today, documents the alliances, rivalries, and motivating interests between senior Séléka leaders and the Chadian and Sudanese governments. It identifies the alliances between senior Séléka leaders and Janjaweed fighters, elephant poachers, and mercenaries from Chad and Sudan. It specifies the resource-rich areas in CAR that are controlled by Anti-Balaka fighters. It describes areas in northeastern provinces near the border with Chad and Sudan that are rich in diamonds and gold and are controlled by Séléka fighters and leaders--including the former CAR president Michel Djotodia, among others. One diamond trader in Bangui told me,

"Séléka needed cash to pay soldiers, to buy food for the soldiers, to get petrol for their vehicles, and to buy arms. The diamond trade helped them to get some of that cash."[1] Senior-level Séléka members and their associates sell diamonds to local traders in CAR or to sellers in Chad, Sudan, Cameroon, and the DRC. Some traders in Bangui claim that considerable amounts of the Séléka diamonds go through South Darfur.[2] The traders and intermediaries then bring the diamonds to trade hubs in South Africa, Belgium, India, Saudi Arabia, Qatar, and the United Arab Emirates.[3]

The findings from my trip also identify the national parks in CAR where mass elephant poaching was ordered or condoned by Séléka leaders as a form of payment for foreign mercenaries. Park rangers from CAR's two northern national parks, Bamingui-Bangoran and Manovo-Gounda Saint Floris, told me, for example, that a group of 70 to 75 Séléka fighters, including former park rangers, attacked the ranger post in Sangba on December 12, 2012. They looted pickup trucks and obtained 24 AK-47 machine guns.[4] The Séléka returned to the area in February 2013 and killed a group of 12 fully grown elephants that had regularly visited areas around the ranger camp.[5] Séléka forces were also responsible for the slaughter of at least 25 elephants in May 2013 at the Dzanga-Sangha Reserve[6] and for the killing of an unknown number of elephants close to Yaloke in February 2013.[7] One interviewee told me that Sudanese poachers supported the Séléka groups by providing weapons and then went to Dzanga-Sangha and Yaloke to kill elephants as payment for their support.[8]

Regional approaches to diplomatic engagement

The connection between natural resources and conflict in CAR became more clear to me as I analyzed the history of security and natural resource-related interests of neighboring countries as well as China, with oil exploration agreements, South Africa, with oil and diamond interests, and France. CAR's northern neighbor, Chad, has particularly keen security and economic interests tied to the Salamat and Doseo oil reserves along the border with CAR. Chadian President Idriss Déby depends heavily on revenues from oil to maintain patronage relationships. He seeks a situation in CAR that denies his opposition a safe haven and allows Chad to retain access to the oil basins on the border, which would decline if CAR began extracting oil.[9] CAR's state fragility and leadership changes affect the Chadian government's calculations about its security. Any developments with exploration or drilling rights could shift alliances among leaders and again destabilize CAR and Chad.

Revenues from oil exploration, diamonds, elephant poaching, and endemic looting in CAR, are directly tied to actors with histories of violence and significant human rights abuses. Investigating these supply chains, identifying the actors who profit from the illicit trade in natural resources, cutting off the financial resources of those who perpetrate violence, and promoting accountability for violence and economic critical activity is crucial.

Congress can help. Congress should urge the Administration to take action on blood diamonds from CAR. The United States and China, as current chair of the Kimberley Process, should work with the Kimberley Process to send review missions to the United Arab Emirates, Belgium, and India to investigate the smuggling of conflict diamonds from CAR. Dubai has not had a Review Mission since 2008 despite numerous reports that diamonds are smuggled through its markets. Review missions and investigations in international diamond trading hubs like that in Dubai could tighten controls and identify individuals and companies against whom the United States and the United Nations could issue targeted sanctions. The

U.S. should also support the U.N. Panel of Experts on CAR and the U.N.-appointed Commission of Inquiry on CAR as they coordinate their efforts to investigate and document economic criminal activity. The U.S. should support efforts by the International Criminal Court in efforts to investigate those most responsible for the violence in CAR, including those involved in sexual violence and economic criminal activity.

CAR's rich natural resources and fragile state institutions have for decades attracted many actors who seek to profit from and also fuel violence that has killed, wounded, and displaced millions. There is an urgent need to recognize the regional implications of these dynamics and the interests of the many transnational actors involved in the illicit trade of natural resources. If U.S. policymakers are able to identify these interests and adopt a regional approach to the diplomatic strategy in CAR, they can play a vital role in the effort to cut off the revenues of violent actors.

Diplomatic engagement and presence

Sustained engagement in any troubled context requires a diplomatic presence that is subject to local security conditions. Discussions about balancing these needs with security for those on the frontlines of foreign service have sparked bitter debates. Some of the most eloquent appeals for expanded diplomatic presence, however, have come from American service officers themselves. I recognize these sensitivities and stand with those who advocate for the reopening of the U.S. Embassy in Bangui, if security conditions allow.

Addressing the acute, immediate needs in CAR, targeting the core drivers of violence, and understanding the interests and revenue sources of mercurial actors with fluid alliances requires sustained on-the-ground diplomatic engagement with a regional perspective and approach. Histories and relationships matter. The deft, skillful, persistent diplomacy by Americans, with Ambassador Symington in the lead, can have a significant and lasting impact in shaping the incentives of those who foment violence.

Recommendations

- **Congress should urge the United Nations to deploy experienced mediators to work with U.S. Special Representative Symington and a diverse group of CAR leaders to spur a bottom-up peace process for CAR.**

- **The Administration should call on the International Criminal Court to prioritize investigations and prosecute those most responsible for the violence in CAR, including those involved in sexual violence and economic criminal activity.**

- **The Administration should work with the African Union to appoint a special envoy to address transnational security and economic matters that involve CAR, Sudan, and Chad.**

- **Congress and the Administration should urge the African Union and United Nations to mediate negotiations between the governments of Chad and CAR on a bilateral agreement for the exploration of the cross-border oilfields between the two states.**

- **Congress should urge the Administration to work with the Kimberley Process to send review missions to the United Arab Emirates, Belgium, and India for investigation into the smuggling of conflict diamonds from CAR.**

- **The U.S. should, if security conditions allow, reopen the embassy in Bangui.**

Conclusion

The United States has led in its response to the intensifying conflict in CAR. Congress has worked hard and consistently to encourage the Administration to take action. With your help, the U.S. has given substantial financial support and helped ensure a transition to a UN Peacekeeping Operation in CAR this September. Several senior diplomats have travelled to the region, including a recent delegation that included Ranking Member Bass. As the U.S. continues to respond to the immediate humanitarian needs of the country's most vulnerable people, the U.S. government must recognize its long-term interests in sustainable peace and stability and work with partners to address the underlying root causes and drivers of conflict. Sustained international attention by the U.S. through a response to financial drivers and economic interests has the potential to make the difference in the struggle for peace.

As U.S. lawmakers chart a path forward on CAR policy, with Ambassador Symington's leadership and engagement, Americans must continue to lead sustainably—with and alongside international partners. The U.S. must press for a bottom-up peace process in CAR. It must work with partners—including the Kimberley Process, the U.N. Commission of Inquiry, and the International Criminal Court—that document, investigate, and pursue accountability for violence and economic criminal activity that sustains violent actors. The U.S. must adopt a regional approach to its diplomacy and engage in a way that recognizes the economic and security interests of a range of actors that have played roles in CAR's troubled history. CAR's most precious resource—its people—deserve nothing less.

---

[1] Diamond trader, interview with author, Bangui, CAR, February 15, 2014.

[2] Diamond trader, interview with author.

[3] Diamond trader, interview with author; Civil servant from CAR Bureau d'Evaluation et de Controle de Diamants et d'Or, interview with author, Bangui, February 21, 2014.

[4] Park rangers and WWF program officer, interviews with author, Bangui, CAR, February 2014.

[5] Park rangers and WWF program officer, interviews with author, Bangui, CAR, February 2014.

[6] WWF program officer and senior civil servants from the CAR Ministry of Forest and Environment, interviews with author, Bangui, CAR,February 2014. See also Laurel Neme, "Chaos and Confusion Following Elephant Poaching in a Central African World Heritage Site," National Geographic News Watch, May 13, 2013, available at http://newswatch.nationalgeographic.com/2013/05/13/chaos-and-confusion-following-elephant-poaching-in-a-central-african-world-heritage-site/.

[7] WWF program officer and senior civil servants from the CAR Ministry of Forest and Environment, interviews with author. See also WWF, "Poachers kill over 11,000 elephants in Gabon," February 6, 2013, available at http://wwf.panda.org/?207520/Poachers-kill-over-11000-elephants-in-Gabon.

[8] Moussa Dhaffane, interview with author.

[9] Senior civil servant in the CAR Ministry of Geology and Mining, interview with author, Bangui, CAR, February 20, 2014. See also Simon Allison, "Conflict of Interest: Chadian peacekeepers may be leaving the Central African Republic, but will the war-torn country ever really be free of its meddling northern neighbor?", *Foreign Policy*, April 9, 2014, available at http://www.foreignpolicy.com/articles/2014/04/09/conflict_of_interest_chad_peacekeepers_car?wp_login_redirect=0.

Mr. SMITH. Thank you so very much as well for your testimony and recommendations.

Ambassador Sanders.

STATEMENT OF THE HONORABLE ROBIN RENEE SANDERS, CHIEF EXECUTIVE OFFICER, FEEEDS ADVOCACY INITIATIVE

Ambassador SANDERS. Thank you, Mr. Chairman and Ranking Member, and members of the subcommittee. I want to thank you for including me in this panel to talk about this very difficult situation.

What my group does is work with diaspora groups around the country, particularly on strategic recommendations, on conflict issues and economic development. I have lived in and worked on Central African regional issues, both when I was Director for Africa at the National Security Council and also when I was U.S. Ambassador to the Republic of the Congo.

The latter time was when former CAR President Bozize first came to power. This was also a time of great conflict and human suffering in CAR. The question the subcommittee is seeking views on today, however, is whether or not the Central African Republic is already in the throes of a pre-genocide atmosphere or already embroiled in genocide. So my remarks will address this and other elements that might be important to consider as we work toward helping CAR as the international community and try to stem the tide of violence that we see today.

I first want to say something that is very similar to what my colleagues on the panel have said about the sheer devastation of the humanitarian crisis. I have been up on the border area many times between Central African Republic and Republic of Congo in my years in the past, and, in fact, there remains refugees there from earlier CAR conflicts.

For more than a decade, military instability and an insecure environment have really been the focus of the CAR environment. It has caused internal issues which have never really been fully resolved. Social issues, political issues, and ethnic issues keep the country environment unstable and the people of the CAR at the mercy of the next wave of violence.

And this has allowed for the rise of what we see today. Because of the continued instability and not being on the radar screen of the international community for more than a decade until the rise of the Seleka in December 2012, the events since then have set in motion two things—revenge killing by the anti-balaka Christian groups, which has now spawned into sectarian violence.

In addition, over the last several days, we are hearing unconfirmed reports of what I would call reverse revenge killing, reportedly from armed Muslim militia of former Seleka running raids from Muslim enclaves in the north into nearby towns, such as attacking 2 days ago a hospital and killing Christians as well as workers with Médecins Sans Frontieres near the border with Chad.

These enclaves only exist because Muslims have been forced to run from sectarian violence directed at them by the anti-balaka groups as well as anti-balaka groups are also preventing those Christians who want to live in peace with their Muslim neighbors from doing so. Therefore, we have, as you know, the following—revenge killing, which has now turned into sectarian violence; a segregated country along Christian-Muslim lines; large numbers of displaced persons afraid and hungry; attacks on convoys evacuating people of either religious group; looming potential for famine and further spread of disease as neither planting or harvesting season has or will take place in the violent environment; and, most importantly, impunity.

You have impunity from the former Seleka and others, including Djotodia and also former President Bozize. These are the elements that could possibly lead down the road to something we have not seen before—a two-way genocide as each group, Muslims and Christians, impose horrendous revenge and reverse revenge killings upon each other.

If we allow this to happen, this would be a new challenge for the country and the international community on top of the already critical humanitarian crisis and thousands of internally displaced persons already on the umbrella of the airport as it is the only place that they feel remotely comfortable.

Thus, what can be suggested as the way forward? I recognize that the administration is working full-time on the humanitarian crisis with internally displaced persons. And as you already are aware, there are many donors that have not stepped up to the plate to provide assistance, both humanitarian-wise as well as with peacekeepers.

The 2,000 French troops and the 5,000 African Union troops of MISCA, as well as the 150 EU troops who have just arrived, should all be commended. But we also need to double down on ensuring that their troops are not seen to support one religious group over another.

Having served in the U.S. Government for many years, I also recognize the timeline needed to get the full complement of the 12,000-person U.N. peacekeeping mission in by September 2014, and that every effort is being made to advance this. But, Mr. Chairman, Ranking Member Bass, the reality may get ahead of their arrival, and we can see that now, particularly if what we are hearing about reverse revenge killing is really taking place with Muslim militia now coming back in and attacking other villages.

Thus, as we balance this triplex of sectarian violence and revenge killings, IDP humanitarian crisis, and looming famine, we may need to jump now to concurrently working with the transitional government and others to set up what we are calling peace groups or peace commissions in rural areas, but particularly in the enclaves and in Bangui, because without a release valve for people to vent and articulate both their fear and hatred, their steep desire to have revenge killings for atrocities done to them or their families, and to address the overall environment of crimes against humanity, the impunity issue, we are likely at the beginning of seeing the current de facto segregation of CAR moving into something worse, such as a two-way genocide, the likes of what we have not seen before.

The potential is there, Mr. Chairman. We can't move to helping people rebuild their lives, restart economic activity, without addressing these issues. In general, peace or reconciliation commissions, such as we have seen in Sierra Leone, South Africa, and even the communal ones that we have seen in Rwanda, generally have begun after peace or at least fragile stability has been restored.

But what we are suggesting here is that these things happen concurrently now, because you have to have a way for a release valve to happen concurrently else you are not going to be able to get to the level of stability that they are trying to seek.

I am not sure we can wait for that phase. As I said, the triplex of issues we see today may prohibit reaching an end to violence and atrocities unless some release valve is actually established. Looking at traditional methods like in Rwanda, what are the traditional methods in CAR to address conflict? I think we need to bring those to the fore, and a lot of the diaspora groups that are here today really have that information for you and have those good ideas.

And I wanted to add something else, and I know this is not directly related to the question of the subcommittee, but I think it is very much an attendant issue. And I would be remiss if I didn't mention this issue after having served as the U.S. Ambassador also in Nigeria, with the resurgence of Boko Haram that has happened there.

Events like we see in CAR, although we might not think that it could get worse, it can. They can spiral even more out of control so quickly and so fast. I think we need to be mindful that there is the potential for untoward groups to come into CAR and take advantage of the unstable environment, and the segregated environment in particular of both Muslims and Christians, not only fueling more hatred and violence but also bringing with them more violent methods, such as terrorist tactics that we haven't yet seen there that could potentially come in.

I am specifically thinking about fundamentalist groups who could come in to provide al-Qaeda-inspired tactics, training in these enclaves because you have segregated societies there.

I think it is important that we pay attention to this, and I want to ensure that my advocacy group, working with other diaspora groups, are really worried about this issue and wanted to bring it to your attention today.

I want to thank the subcommittee again for allowing me to share these views, and I am happy to address your questions. I would also like to submit my revised remarks, with your permission, to the committee.

[The prepared statement of Ambassador Sanders follows:]

Testimony before the Subcommittee on Africa and Global Health, Global Human Rights, and International Organizations

May 1, 2014

Subject of Hearing: Central African Republic – State of Affairs: Pre-Genocide or Genocide

Ambassador Robin Renee Sanders (ret), CEO FEEEDS Advocacy Initiative

Mr. Chairman, Ranking Member, and members of the Committee, I want to thank you for including me on this panel on the situation in the Central Africa Republic (CAR), and issue that I am following very closely. I have lived in and work on Central African regional issues both when I was a Director for Africa at the National Security Council and also when I was U.S. Ambassador to the Republic of Congo. The latter time was when former CAR President Bozizé first came to power; this was also a time of great conflict and human suffering in CAR. The question the Committee is seeking views on today, however, is whether or not the Central African Republic is already in the throes of a pre-genocide atmosphere or already embroiled in genocide. My remarks will address this and other elements that might be important to consider as we work together as the international community to try to stem the tide of violence and human suffering in CAR.

I first want to say something about the sheer devastation of the humanitarian crisis, having been up on the border area many times between Central Africa Republic (CAR) and Republic of Congo in years past, and in fact there remain refugees there from earlier CAR conflicts. For more than a decade instability has reigned in CAR caused by internal issues which have never been fully resolved – socially, politically, and ethnically – keeping the country environment unstable, and the people of the CAR at the mercy of the next wave of violence. Because of the continued instability and not being on the radar screen of the international community for more than a decade until the rise of the Seleka in December 2012, the events since then have set in motion two things: revenge killing by the anti-balaka Christian groups, which has now spawned into sectarian violence.

In addition over the last several days we are hearing unconfirmed reports of what I have been calling "reverse revenge killings" reportedly from armed Muslim militias or former Seleka running raids from Muslim enclaves in the North into nearby towns such as attacking two days ago a hospital, and killing Christians, and workers with Medicine San Frontier, near the border with Chad. These enclaves only exist because Muslims have been forced to run from sectarian violence directed at them by the anti-balaka groups. Anit-balaka groups also are preventing those Christians who want to live in peace with their Muslim neighbors from doing so.

Therefore, what we have, as you know, are the following:

- Sectarian violence;

- Segregated country along Christian-Muslim lines;
- Large numbers of displaced person, afraid and facing hunger
- Attacks on convoys evacuating people of either religious groups
- Looming potential for famine and further spread of disease as neither planting or harvesting season has or will take place in the violent environment

These are elements that could possibly lead down the road to something we have not seen before:

- A two-way genocide as each group, Muslim and Christians, impose horrendous revenge and "reverse revenge" killing upon each other.

If we allow this to happen this will be a new challenge for the country and international community on top of the already critical humanitarian crisis with thousands of internally displaced persons (IDP's) already on the umbrella of the airport as it is the only place they feel remotely safe.

Thus, what can be suggested as the way forward? I recognize that the Administration is working full time on the humanitarian crisis with internally displaced person, but other donors also need to step up and fulfill pledges to provide assistance. The 2,000 French troops and the 5,000 African Union troops of MISCA as well as the 150 EU troops who have just arrived should all be commended, but also we need to double down on ensuring that their troops are not seen to support one religious group over another.

Having served in government for many years, I also recognize the time line needed to get the full complement of the 12,000-person UN Peace Keeping Mission in by September 2014 and that every effort is being made to advance this. But, the reality may get ahead of their arrival – and, we can see this now if we are entering a new phase of reverse revenge killings by Muslim militia.

Thus, as we balance this ***triplex*** of sectarian violence/revenge killings, the IDP humanitarian crisis, and looming famine we may need to jump now to *concurrently* work with the transition government to setup Peace Commission in rural areas and in Bangui because without a release valve for people to vent and articulate both their fear and hatred; stem their desire to revenge kill for atrocities done to them or their families, and address the overall environment of crimes against humanity we are likely at the beginning of seeing the current de facto segregation of CAR move into something worse - such as a two-way genocide the likes of which we have not seen before. The potential is there.

In general peace or reconciliation commissions such as in Sierra Leone, South Africa, and even the communal ones in Rwanda began in after peace – or at least fragile stability - had been restored, or in the case of South Africa when apartheid had been abolished.

I am not sure we can wait for that phase in CAR. The triplex of issues we see today may prohibit reaching an end to violence and atrocities unless some release value for the hatred and disregard for humanity by the militia groups on both sides is addressed concurrently in the present environment.

Although this is not directly part of the Committee's question today, I would be remiss if I didn't mention this issue having served as U.S. Ambassador also in Nigeria when the resurgence of Boko Haram happened. Events like we see in CAR, although we might think it cannot get worse, it can. They can spirally even more out of control so quickly, so fast. Thus, I think we need to be mindful that there is the potential for untoward groups to come into CAR and take advantage of the environment and the segregated environment of Muslims and Christians – not only fueling more hatred and violence, but also bringing with them more violent method such as terrorist tactics. I am specifically thinking of fundamentalist groups who could come in to provide Al-Qaeda-inspired terrorist training to help advance the mission of revenge and reverse revenge killings. This could happen on either side of the religious divide, not just within the Muslim segregated enclaves but also within segregated Christian segregated communities that now exist since the negative atmosphere of hatred and violent pay-back is the order of the day. We need to pay attention to this and seek to work as much as possible within these enclaves to not only distribute much-needed food, but find ways with these groups to create the space for the revenge killings to end on both sides.

Again, I want to thank the Subcommittee for Again for allowing me to share these views.

Mr. SMITH. Without objection, Ambassador Sanders, yours and all of the other full statements will be made a part of the record. Thank you for your testimony.

Ms. Bass has another appointment pressing, so I yield to Ms. Bass.

Ms. BASS. Thank you, Mr. Chair. I appreciate your flexibility. And I want to thank all of the panelists, and I appreciate your contributions.

I did want to ask before I have to leave, Ambassador Sanders, if you could just expand a little more. For example, you were talking about the reconciliation process beginning now. And you mentioned, you know, several different countries. You also mentioned looking at the traditional processes that happen.

So are you suggesting now that reach-out begin to the various countries—South Africa, Rwanda, Sierra Leone—and that teams are put together to come into the country now? And do you know if the AU or anybody else is attempting to do that?

Ambassador SANDERS. As far as I know right now, Congresswoman Bass, no one is attempting to do that. I know these are ideas that have germinated within the diaspora community. I did hear our colleague from CRS mention the workshops. But what we are talking about is something a little bit different than that because really going into the enclaves and having discussions now in these segregated communities.

And I think it is important that we look at traditional ways of arbitration similar to what Rwanda did. So we need to find out what those traditional ways of arbitrations have been in the CAR context with their respective ethnic groups, because sometimes those ways of arbitration are quite different from ethnic group to ethnic group.

And we need to start working with those groups in-country as well as look at outside examples and bring those in. I heard Rwanda mentioned earlier, but there are other examples out there too. And I think Sierra Leone I think is a really good example that is even similar to the situation in CAR, given the extent of the atrocities both in Rwanda and in Sierra Leone. I think those are two good examples.

Ms. BASS. Well, I know that you are going to be leaving soon. But when you come back, I would like to continue conversations about this and maybe look as to how we make that concrete. So thank everyone very much for your testimony.

Ambassador SANDERS. Thank you, Congresswoman Bass.

Mr. SMITH. Thank you, Ms. Bass.

Just a few questions. And, again, I thank you for your patience with all of the interruptions with voting.

You know, I am concerned that there seems to be—maybe we have it now, but there has been a lack of urgency. I mean, last July many of us were raising these issues in earnest. I know that Bishop Nongo, when he came and testified, he was fresh from coming from the United Nations at which he tried, in talking to permanent representatives there, especially Security Council members, he had a sense of urgency that not only were the killing fields horrific then, that they could quickly become, you know, another Rwanda. And he made that point very clear, as he testified here.

And yet the U.N. punted for weeks, now months, and now they seem to be standing up a force. I did ask Ambassador Jackson earlier about, you know, when the deployment actually occurs and we are still months away from that even though there is some augmentation going on of certain troops.

And then we are still not sure, because I did ask him and I would appreciate any thoughts you have on this, about the configuration of the force, especially if it is right-sized and not being driven by how much money potentially will be in the kitty to fund it, but what is necessary to do the job and to do it as effectively as possible.

I mean, were the Pentagon and others involved in this? Because it would seem to me that, you know, we do have planners who know what it takes. And very often—and we have seen this over and over again all over the world, despite the—you know, the goodwill of the blue helmets, but if they don't have the right mandate, and if they don't have enough people, it doesn't happen.

And I mentioned earlier about Srebrenica, you know, the safe haven cities and a force that had horrible, and I mean horrible, rules of engagement. Just parenthetically, I had the translator who met with the Dutch peacekeepers in Mladic testify here soon after all of the Muslim men were slaughtered in Srebrenica, and he said he couldn't believe it. The peacekeepers were handing over the men to slaughter, and we have seen that replicated, in whole or in part, all over the world.

So my point would be, are we moving with the urgency, with sufficient resources? You, Ms. Rose, point out in your testimony, your first two points—and all of you have said this—the importance of a robust force security and all the rest, but then you even talk about the humanitarian part. The 2014 global humanitarian appeal is only 28 percent funded, three-quarters not funded.

You point out that the first priority for Congress, and I thank you for underscoring that to Members of Congress, to be protecting appropriations funding for the international disaster assistance and migration and refugee assistance accounts to ensure humanitarian needs can be met throughout 2014 and into 2015.

Then, you point out ominously and disappointingly that the administration's 2015 budget request to Congress cuts the international disaster assistance funds for displaced persons by 28 percent from 2014 levels, and the MRA account by 33 percent. You also, as has been said throughout this hearing, other donors, other countries, need to be stepping up to the plate as well and meeting their obligations.

And, Madam Ambassador, you might want to speak to this, too, because you were on the inside for so long. How do we get the administration itself, and then, by extension, Congress, to realize that this crisis is being underfunded? And we do take our cues from the administration. I have been in Congress 34 years. When an administration lays out a number that they think is the requisite amount for disaster assistance, for example, it does become a very important number that is taken seriously. It is not something we just throw over the side, and to up it takes a lot of data and information that you in the NGO community especially, and as experts, can help us.

So I think your admonishment to us to meet this unmet need, particularly in the budget that has been proffered by the administration, is a very serious shortfall on the part of the administration. So you might want to speak to that as well.

And, finally, I just want to ask—I do have a lot of questions, but if you would touch on those. The work of Catherine Samba-Panza, you know, the sense from the testimony is that there was a heightened sense of expectation and hopefulness that may have been diminished over the last several weeks. Is that true? Does she have the kind of backstopping that she needs by the international community as head of state?

And, finally, when it comes to children's issues, what are the kids doing? I mean, I appreciate, Mr. Campbell, you talked about that one individual who decided not to go the route of the gun simply because you in your workshops had inspired him to see another route to take. But, you know, there are a lot of young youth, young people I should say, and especially the most vulnerable, the under-five part of the population and vulnerable women who are not getting the kind of help that they need, particularly in this crisis situation, maternal mortality, child mortality—you mentioned, Ambassador, about, you know, famine and further spread of disease—you know, the stalking of a whole slew of diseases that could break out, if they haven't already, if you could speak to that as well because these are all issues that it helps us to know with as many specifics as possible, so that we can respond accordingly, particularly with the resources.

Madam Ambassador, I understand you will have to leave shortly, so if you wouldn't mind going first.

And I would ask my friend and colleague, Mr. Meadows, if he might have a question for the Ambassador as well, so that he can get his question in to you before you have to make your departure.

Ambassador SANDERS. Okay. Let me take the right-sizing issue first, because I think that's a really extremely important one. And we should have learned lessons I think from Rwanda, which should be applied here. I think that you are absolutely right that U.S. planners should be involved in this, and they can be working with the U.N. Department of Peacekeeping Operations to really make sure we have got it right this time in terms of the—not only the force size but the elements of the force, so that you are really not only addressing the peacekeeping mechanism but maybe in addition to the policing mechanism as well, because you have got to have the space for security, but you also have to have the policing, so that you can maintain or keep the security that you have gained, because every time the peacekeepers move to a different location, then you have a fallback of that previously protected area that is no longer protected.

So I think we should have learned lessons from Rwanda in terms of better managing the numbers and making sure we have the right-sizing done. And I think more dialogue with our planners and the Department of Peacekeeping Operations at the U.N., I think really needs to be done, so we can get those numbers right this time, and get the mix right, because we may need more police than we need peacekeepers or the various combinations. But definitely you need both types of forces on the ground.

In terms of the interim President, first of all, let me take my hat off to her because she is definitely trying to manage a very, very difficult situation, and I think she needs all of the support the international community can provide to her. But I would add that some of the examples that have been provided by my colleagues here, including the idea of possibly having these peace groups or peace commissions begin, I think we really need to start working with her and the transitional government in order to make that happen, because they have to have buy-in, too.

We can't—we are not able to do these things without the buy-in of the transitional government as well. So we have to get her buy-in on some of these ideas that have been presented to the sub-committee, so that we are working in lockstep and not in counter-step with each other.

In terms of the famine and disease, you heard earlier about World Food Programme's stats on what they have in terms of what they are able to provide to the IDPs. But you are also missing the other point in terms of normally you have a planting and a harvest season. That hasn't taken place because of the violence. So the normal foodstocks that are there are also diminished. So in addition to having a reduced amount of relief food, you also have a reduced amount of the normal stocks that are in CAR.

So I am worried about the potential for famine for both reasons, and I think that this is something that our administration needs to look at down the line maybe 3 or 4 months, because we could be having this same conversation in August and September, quite differently as we are facing famine on top of an already bad situation.

Mr. SMITH. The cut that has been proposed, would that be devastating, that Ms. Rose mentioned in her testimony, the cut to the international disaster relief account? It is a huge cut.

Ambassador SANDERS. She is absolutely right. That is going to impact everybody's ability to do their job, particularly on the humanitarian side. So we can't diminish any of these things. I mentioned earlier that we had a triplex of issues that we haven't had before, and all of these are converging and that is a big one. And it would also help address the famine—the potential famine issue down the line as well.

Ms. ROSE. Thank you, Chairman. I will just go down the line, if that's okay, with some of the questions.

Mr. SMITH. Please.

Ms. ROSE. So in the MINUSCA mandate, I think from Mercy Corps' perspective we don't have a position on the numbers, but we are happy with the mandate. We think it has a very strong, well thought out mandate that is intentionally chronologically strategic about what it is supposed to achieve. So it starts with a clear intent to protect civilians and then transitions into the state-building and institution-building down the line, which we think is smart and isn't always laid out.

We are also really happy with language that requires MINUSCA to work with humanitarian and human rights partners in devising a comprehensive protection strategy from the get-go as it scales up, which is kind of new and innovative language, and we think really critical about—that means the U.N. is going to have to allocate resources to do an entire risk assessment of protection concerns throughout the country, and then plan a strategic response, which is really good.

I think what is kind of below that, which is more important, is that, you know, we have to support MISCA, which we have all stated and you well know. But it kind of answers the first question about MINUSCA, because the fluidity of the crisis in CAR is so constant. It changes every day. There are new threats emerging in different parts of the country, and so the focus should really be on reinforcing MISCA, which we have some recommendations for that I think I said in my testimony. But I think that's the priority.

Third, on the funding question and how disastrous it would be, I think it would be really great for, you know, the administration to feel some pressure from Congress and for Congress to request a conversation or a briefing from the administration their rationale behind those cuts and how they think we are going to respond not just in CAR but in South Sudan and Syria where these displacement and protracted situations are not getting better. I think that would be a good initiative.

But I also want to underscore that the fact that we have to keep fighting for crisis response underscores the fact that we aren't investing enough in prevention. These crises are expensive. They get more and more expensive the longer that they unravel, yet in our foreign assistance budget we have very few mechanisms available for proactive prevention.

The Complex Crisis Fund is one—the USAID Complex Crisis Fund is one of the newest tools that was developed in 2010. It is funding Catholic Relief Services, Search for Common Ground, and Mercy Corps—they were able to respond very quickly. They turned around a proposal in, you know, a matter of weeks. That is a great tool that we really think should be scaled up to at least $100 million, and beyond just the CCF and rapid response structures, but really finding—looking at our foreign assistance priorities and platforms and how we can carve out more proactive prevention.

On your question of Samba-Panza and the transitional government, from my perceptions on the ground and from our staff's perceptions, there still is faith and optimism in the transitional government, but it is waning as we mentioned. And what we really prioritize is that the transitional government has a support package to pay civil salaries and to restore basic state functions, so that they can begin to provide services.

We are happy with The World Bank's announcement earlier this week, which will be an initial salary payment, but it is very small. We also think the IMF really needs to get involved, and we recently heard that they plan to send their assessment team in July, which we think is not fast enough. And if Congress could help accelerate that process for their scale-up grant, it would be really great.

Fifth, on the question of vulnerable populations and the displacement crisis, there have been a lot of comparisons of CAR to Rwanda. But what I was trying to sort of portray in my testimony, and what we are really seeing is that it is actually we think unfolding into something more like a DRC, where there is a massive protracted displacement crisis. And if the international community is distracted and only responds to the immediate needs without thinking of the underlying root causes that caused the conflict in the first place, that we are going to end up having to spend billions of dollars for 20 years and still have a crisis.

And that is why we are encouraging long-term investments in state-building and institution-building and political reconciliation, so that we don't see CAR fall into a similar crisis down the line.

And just quickly on reconciliation, which Ms. Bass asked about, there are some local initiatives going on already on reconciliation. But a lot of the local structures have been completely destroyed, so there is really a need to invest and scale those up, but there are local capacities that can begin.

There is also high-level engagement on political reconciliation, so the U.N. Mediation Support Unit has been working on a reconciliation plan. MINUSCA Political Affairs, their primary task over the next 3 months is to find all the different influencers and the power players and to start to rebuild that strategy and so I think the big key for Congress is to stay engaged with that process and see where there are gaps and where there is need for support, and to ensure that that reconciliation process is coordinated, so that the local efforts and the high-level efforts are coordinated and go in parallel to make sure that you don't loose the connection between the grassroots and the elites in society, which for so long hasn't been there and that is a big undercurrent of the crisis.

Mr. AGGER. Yes. Thank you so much once again. I would say that the important point I think here, it is not just a matter of how many troops we get. And for me personally, I am not a military planner, so I can't talk much about that. But I think what all of us have said here on the panel is that the political process has stalled, and the transitional government, there is still hope, yes, but her ability to deliver is very limited, because she has no army, she has no police. There are no judges. She does not have a state budget at the moment.

So her ability to respond to international and to local expectations is extremely limited. So I think that is where the international community needs to come in and provide her some tools to help her. You can provide her with finance. You can provide her with advisors and support to bring out the political mandate.

And then I think, secondly, the reconciliation process, as everybody has talked about, needs to start now from the bottom up at the grassroots level, because you have all of these different armed groups that are operating without any central command in different parts of the country. So you can't just call the usual suspects of the key leaders of Seleka and anti-balaka who sit in the capital, Bangui, and try to have a roundtable and solve it that way.

You need to create a team of negotiators or advisors that can actually travel around the country and start to distill what the local issues are and start to broker some local understandings, because I agree very much with my colleague here that once the dialogue starts—and I think that is what you also heard from the representatives who were here from the religious community last year—that it is possible to reconcile people, but it is not happening at the moment.

Thank you.

Mr. CAMPBELL. I would agree that the new interim President and the government is not given the support it needs to really make an impact. They are losing credibility every minute of the day. In fact, Bishop Nestor, when he was in Bangui, I went to the mass where the President had attended as well, and he was very clear.

The police and the army of the country itself has no arms. They are not part of this process, and he had made the point that that had been the case in Sierra Leone, Ivory Coast, and other places as well. So the population that is supposed to be part of rebuilding the government and the society are not even involved in the process.

With regard to support, I think I see it in three different ways, and it is support, which has been slow to the humanitarian situation, the security, and, again, as I said, the interim government. They cannot move forward, and they lose that credibility with the population and undermine the very governance that got us into this problem over the past several decades.

Regarding the workshops and reconciliation, in fact, we do work in those enclaves, and that needs to be expanded and, I agree with my colleagues, coordinated. But it has to involve the people of the country itself and cascade down throughout the communities. It is not something that can be helicoptered in, but our work is very much with those faith leaders, but also community leaders, parliamentarians, they have to take hold of the process of reconciliation and the social fabric.

Thank you.

Mr. SMITH. Thank you.

Mr. Meadows.

Mr. MEADOWS. Thank you, Mr. Chairman, and for continuing to bring this issue to the center and forefront of not only our minds but to many of our colleagues. Sadly, for many of the people we represent, if you were to ask them to find the CAR on a map, they could not do it. And yet the atrocities that are happening daily are things that they would find appalling.

And so your testimony here today is critical because it sheds some light on it. My concern is is at times we take this—and many of you live and breathe this every single day, so you know the subtleties of it, you know what works, what doesn't work. And yet when you come to testify, you paint a very broad-brush picture of what you would like to see the CAR look like maybe 10, 20 years from now, knowing full well that it only will happen in very small incremental stages. But we have, from what I am hearing, we have a critical timeline that must be addressed both financially and with other resources immediately. Is that correct? So all of you are nodding yes.

So your testimony—so let me go further. I assumed that that would be a yes from all four of you. So let me go further, because I am putting this in several different buckets. One is humanitarian. One is peacekeeping. But the other is something that the Ambassador alluded to, and I guess, Mr. Campbell, you alluded to as well, is the policing side of that to even provide for a peaceful situation so that reconciliation, so that economic growth, a number of those things can take place.

How do we best assist, recognizing the sovereign nation, you know, and the sovereignty of a foreign government, to come in where it is not the United States trying to put their particular stamp on a country and a culture that we really don't want to Americanize. How do we get, one, that message across? And, two, how do we very quickly on the policing side of it assist? Because if you look to train police and military, that is a very long process. It does not happen in a month or two.

So it almost requires intervention. What is the best solution to that? So that the peacekeeping can indeed do the peacekeeping, Madam Ambassador, as you mentioned, recognizing we have limited resources. But how do we best set the priority for what we do first to start this process? And, Madam Ambassador, I know you need to leave, so I will start with you.

Ambassador SANDERS. Thank you so much. I think your points are extremely important. One of the things that I think that can be done on the U.N. side, because policing can be done with a U.N. mandate as well, if they include it in the mandate, and so your timeline about training, yes, that is down the line for people of CAR, but to bring in police as part of the U.N. mandate would not be unheard of. And you can do that to solidify whatever gains you do make in terms of security. So that is one way to at least start, by including bringing in police units as part of the U.N. peace-keeping effort.

So you can build on the police that are there to at least establish or begin to establish security units that can go and travel and try to maintain the areas that have already been secured, or that need to be resecured and maintain those, and look at training the CAR police way down the line.

Mr. MEADOWS. So is that something that the current government would welcome, or, I mean, what—politically, what would we have there?

Ambassador SANDERS. I think that it is something that, given the fact that the transitional government needs a lot of support, I think it is something that they would welcome, because they understand the fact that without that kind of constant security that they are never going to be able to reach their goal or the goal of the international community to provide stability for CAR.

So I do think it is something that they would consider positively, and I think it is something that we need to think about and actually encourage the U.N. to take a look at, including inviting police units as part of the U.N. force to be in CAR.

One of the areas that you didn't mention that I really think we haven't spent enough time on is the impunity issue. And I say that because part of that reconciliation is for people to be able to see that the international community has taken the question of impunity very, very seriously, and that is with former Seleka leaders, that is with former President Bozize and others. And we haven't really addressed that as the international community as of yet, and I——

Mr. MEADOWS. So with a marginal judicial system within the CAR, I mean, so how do you do that? I mean, how functionally do you have that impunity where it gets dealt with?

Ambassador SANDERS. Well, we do have the International Criminal Court. That is one of the reasons that the International Criminal Court is there when an internal system cannot deal with crimes against humanity itself. And so that is a mechanism, that is an area where we can at least begin that dialogue and have the ICC look at this question of impunity of some of the leaders that are out there, some of those that have caused the current violence, and some of them that are responsible for the underlying causes that are in CAR today.

So I think it is something we can do. The International Criminal Court is there, and that is part of one of its mandates is to look at issues where the country itself cannot manage its own judicial system in a way that you can address the question of impunity.

Mr. MEADOWS. So can you comment, if you would for me, on the Atrocities Prevention Board, how that has either played in, or doesn't play in, or what role does it play in the CAR at this point. Can anybody comment on that?

Ambassador SANDERS. There may be others that are best placed, but we heard earlier today that as far as the administration understood maybe there was one meeting, but there may be others on the panel that might be better placed to answer that than I am.

Mr. MEADOWS. Ms. Rose, I see they are all looking at you. [Laughter.]

Ms. ROSE. I am excited for this question. So from our perspective, so as an NGO community that has collectively worked on mass atrocities prevention advocacy, in our opinion, we do think that the Atrocities Prevention Board played a very important role.

For the comments that the State Department didn't know about the CAR crisis until November and December, I thought that was a problematic response and that there is some potential opportunity for Congress to push back and ask how that is possibly the case, given that the——

Mr. MEADOWS. Potential opportunity, right?

Ms. ROSE [continuing]. That I would love for you to use.

Mr. MEADOWS. I did of did ask, but I will ask——

Ms. ROSE. Right. But follow up and say, you know, if the coup happened in March, and we now have interagency structures to raise red flags up the ladder to the highest level, how is it possible that the State Department wasn't looking at this intentionally in November and December? So I think that is a follow-up opportunity.

But the Atrocities Prevention Board, from our perspective, did play an important role. They were convening behind-the-scenes meetings. The Conflict Stabilization Office, out of the State Department, was the key locus of sharing information across the interagency. In August, September, October, and November, they did convene meetings. They had open sessions with the NGO partners, so we could express what we were seeing. So that would not have happened with out the Atrocities Prevention Board and Presidential Study Directive 10.

That said, clearly, we were too late. So our question that, again, we would love for Congress to ask is, what happened in March? And where does atrocities prevention sit on parallel with other national intelligence priorities?

Mr. MEADOWS. Right.

Ms. ROSE. If CAR was, you know, geopolitically strategically irrelevant until mass atrocities were occurring, how are we better elevating that prioritization framework? And how can we get ahead of—how can we pay better attention to——

Mr. MEADOWS. So how do we put a better emphasis ahead of the curve instead of after the curve, is that correct?

Ms. ROSE. Yes.

Mr. MEADOWS. Okay.

Ms. ROSE. In 2013, out of Presidential Study Directive 10, they were required to create a National Intelligence Estimate on mass atrocity threats everywhere in the world. It is not public obviously, but that, we understand, has been created. And so, you know, figuring out where CAR was on that list, how it moved, I think CAR would be a really great case study for Congress and the interagency to explore where the breakdowns are in that system.

But we do think that there has been progress, and that because of the APB's existence, because of Presidential Study Directive 10, because of the core U.S. commitment to preventing mass atrocities, the response was faster than it ever would have been.

And quickly I would just add where we think there needs to be more progress moving forward, one would be unlocking the information-sharing problem and these blockages to investing and more flexible and long-term funding across the board, recognizing that you can't solve CAR's crises and challenges in 12 months. We need multi-year assistance programs that let practitioners and implementers really deal with the complexities of these problems. And then, third would be to codify our commitments in law to mass atrocities prevention.

So under PSD–10, you know, that might not live beyond the Obama administration unless Congress codifies it into law, and that would be great.

Mr. MEADOWS. All right. So let me kind of bring it down. If we were to only do two things in the next 90 days, what would it be? Two things. Now, I know that, you know, we need humanitarian and we need policing and all of that. But if we could only do two things and say that this is the most critical time because we are underfunded, we are understaffed, we are, you know, what would it be—I was at a dinner, and I can tell you that whether it is NGOs, the State Department, the U.N., a number of them, the focus for them was two places, South Sudan and the CAR.

And that was the focus, and they were saying we have got to act, and we have got to act immediately. But for every day that we don't act, there are lives that are being lost. And so how do we do this—if we were to say the next 90 days you could do anything that you wanted to do, what would it do in terms of, how would you prioritize our involvement there? Mr. Campbell, we will start with you.

Mr. CAMPBELL. Security would be first, because we need that operating environment.

Mr. MEADOWS. And by ''security,'' do you mean policing or peacekeeping or——

Mr. CAMPBELL. If I can get away with it, I will take both.

Mr. MEADOWS. But if you had just one, what would it be?

Mr. CAMPBELL. The security, meaning not the police but—because the situation is so volatile that until that is stabilized, nothing else can move.

Mr. MEADOWS. Okay.

Mr. CAMPBELL. And then, secondly, the humanitarian response, because people are in such need, particularly food security over and above the—before you get to the immediate response. That has to come, but this is—because of how this has evolved, this is a long-term disaster, particularly with food security. As I said earlier, this is 2 years of consecutive problems with planting, and so forth. Even in the lean periods before the crisis, it was very difficult.

Mr. MEADOWS. Sure. Okay.

Ms. Rose?

Ms. ROSE. I would concur that the first initiative would be to reinforce MISCA. They are specifically trying to find replacement 850 peacekeepers for the Chadian force that left, but also just explore across the interagency if there are ways for the United States to increase assistance to MISCA in the immediate term.

And then, number two would be to pass a bill authorizing multiyear assistance funding to CAR that transcends the regular appropriations calendar, so that not just financial assistance but it would be a 4- or 5-year strategic response bill that includes humanitarian development, diplomatic and political commitments to seeing CAR through its transition.

Mr. MEADOWS. All right. What I would like is, if you would—and not for open testimony, but if you would submit what that budget would look like, what the parameters. I don't need a Cadillac or a Rolls Royce version. I won't mention another vehicle, but I need something less than that. [Laughter.]

How about that? Okay?

Ms. ROSE. Yes, sir.

Mr. MEADOWS. Mr. Agger?

Mr. AGGER. Yes. Thank you. I would agree that those are critical issues, but I would like to propose that we look—think a little bit outside the box and not just think about more troops and more police. I firmly believe that with local dialogues, a reconciliation approach, we will be able to contain the violence. It is another method to stop the violence that has not been tried in the country. And I firmly believe that it will make a huge difference on the ground once people start to talk together.

Mr. MEADOWS. Okay. What would be their motivation to talk?

Mr. AGGER. Their motivation is that nobody really has a good situation. People are displaced. People are being attacked daily. So my experience from talking to local people, people are seeking leadership and seeking guidance. They are seeking someone who will try to put order in place. And I believe that it is much more cost effective to start local dialogues than to keep pushing for additional peacekeeping forces. And, realistically speaking, I just don't see where the finances and the troops going are to come from at this moment.

Mr. MEADOWS. All right. Let me follow up, and then we will let you finish, because I know we are pressing on time limits for everybody. You mentioned diamonds and a few of the other things and outside influences. What component or what percentage of this is a terrorist, organized crime intervention within that in terms of diamonds and other natural resources? Whether it be Hezbollah or any of the others, what kind of presence would you see them having in the CAR?

Mr. AGGER. It is not something we have seen to date. What we have seen is that particularly the Seleka alliance and key members used ivory poaching and control of diamond areas to finance the rebel group. And most of those commodities went through Sudan, because of the strong relations with the Sudanese Government and members of the Janjaweed militia.

So I think that is where we would have to look, but I recognize these are more long-term issues that will not have an immediate effect. That is why I do not raise it as the most crucial point.

Mr. MEADOWS. Okay. Madam Ambassador?

Ambassador SANDERS. Thank you. I also have to echo police and peace and security as number one, and I think you can't split the two. You need both police and security. But I am going to go back to the impunity issue, because I think it is double-sided. One, because it shows if you bring leadership to the justice system, then you have a better chance of reconciliation happening on the ground.

If people see that the leaders of Seleka or former President Bozize and others that have looted and put the country in the situation that it is now are being brought to justice, I think that it better helps the reconciliation process on the ground. Again, I go back——

Mr. MEADOWS. So that becomes the motivation for them to talk, as Mr. Agger was talking about, if they can't operate without impunity.

Ambassador SANDERS. Right. Exactly. If you have the leadership that is operating with impunity, then, you know, what is the motivation, you are right, even if we have more peace groups. I think it encourages people when they see that the leadership is also brought to justice that they have a better chance of survival. And so I would encourage that we begin a dialogue with the ICC to look possibly at the CAR and bringing some of these leaders—leadership to justice.

And, lastly, and it was touched on briefly, is the complicity issue by various elements throughout the region. I do think that that has historically been a problem with CAR. You do have, you know, various complicity support coming from different countries around CAR and what their role is, whether it is on the economic resource side or whether it is on the political influence side.

Those two issues have existed for more than a decade in terms of outside complicity, helping to destabilize CAR, and that has not changed. So we need to bring our administration's voice and the voice of Congress to some of those leaders around the region, and address some of the complicity issues that we all know are there.

Mr. MEADOWS. Mr. Chairman, I appreciate your patience. I yield back.

Mr. SMITH. Thank you very much.

Just before we conclude, just a couple of final questions, especially as it relates to the ICC. Yesterday in this room the full Foreign Affairs Committee passed my resolution that I introduced way back in September and held a hearing on and did an op-ed for the

Washington Post on the need for a Syrian war crimes tribunal that would be patterned after an ad hoc, similar to what we had in Sierra Leone, Rwanda, and the former Yugoslavia.

The ICC, as we all know, has had one conviction in over a decade. It has 18 investigations, all Africans, nobody else for some odd reason. And it seems to have all kinds of internal constraints. A lot of it has to do with the way it was configured, that makes it less flexible, doesn't go after as many people, does not have a chilling effect.

And one of the things that David Crane said when he testified, the chief prosecutor for Sierra Leone who sat right where you all sit just a few months ago, was that—you know, and he gave a number of scenarios of what that ad hoc tribunal would look like, but you have got to have the ability to go after both sides. You have to have the ability to go after more than one actor or, you know, one or two, which is what the ICC often does. And, again, only 18 indictments in over a dozen years is not a record that gives a lot of hope that they will have any consequence here.

So my question would be, should we be looking at an ad hoc tribunal as it relates to the CAR? Similar to what we are trying to get off the ground for Syria.

And, secondly, Ms. Rose, you mentioned and talked about targeted interventions toward protecting women. Several years ago, I don't know if you know this, but I actually am the author of the Trafficking Victims Protection Act, our landmark law in combatting sex and labor trafficking.

Well, Greg Simpkins, our staff director on the subcommittee, and I learned quite horrifyingly that peacekeepers in DR Congo were raping little girls. Here are the peacekeepers, with a duty to protect, with a mandate to protect, had not been properly vetted, and were actually raping little girls.

So we held three hearings on it. The U.N. did issue a zero tolerance policy to its credit and did some good work, at least on paper, and some tried to do it for real. But we went there and visited not only the peacekeepers but also a place called HEAL Africa, where so many women who had been gang raped by armed individuals, as you pointed out in your testimony, were getting a faith-based approach that were helping them get their lives back, to deal with a trauma that is unthinkable and yet they were getting some real help.

Juxtapose that, and to you, Ambassador Sanders, is it a problem in Nigeria. Is it a problem of trafficking in CAR? We haven't heard much about that. Have peacekeepers been complicit in any way?

Just the other day we heard of all of those young women, students, being trafficked by Boko Haram in Nigeria, and there have been marches in Abuja about it, because people are frustrated. And those young girls were sold into slavery, abducted and now sold into slavery by Boko Haram.

And I am wondering if anything like that is happening in CAR. Have there been any reports of trafficking? And are we all making sure that those peacekeepers that are deployed and will be deployed are properly vetted so that they don't become part of the problem rather than part of the solution? My final question.

Ambassador SANDERS. Thank you, Mr. Chairman. On the question of whether it should be an ICC or an ad hoc tribunal, I think that the bigger, macro issue is the impunity. Whether it is a tribunal or whether we do a one-off at the ICC, I think it is the message that it sends and the vehicle that we choose I think—I think both vehicles will be useful because you do have the international aspect from the ICC.

You are right on the number of convictions, but at least it brings an international zero-in on the impunity issue as well as you could probably do a war crimes tribunal as well. But I think it is the question of impunity. I haven't heard specifically on trafficking, but let me just say that I would not be surprised if that is also an underlying issue that is going on. And if it hasn't started, there is always the potential with instability like that for that to become another unfortunate weapon of war of trafficking young men and women in that circumstance.

So I think that is another thing you are absolutely right to put on the table, and it is one thing that we have to watch.

In fact, I am headed to Nigeria right now to go to Kano and Katsina, and so I don't know if I will be allowed to—my flight leaves at 2:30. So if that is okay, thank you so much.

Mr. AGGER. Yes. Thank you so much again. I will talk to the issue of the peacekeepers. There have been several incidents where Chadian peacekeepers have been involved in violent acts against civilians. The event we talked about earlier today where 30 civilians were killed, that was perpetrated by Chadian soldiers. Some of them were even special forces soldiers that were operating without any mandate inside the country, which is just horrible and needs much more international scrutiny to prevent these events in the future.

And I would also just take this opportunity to say that I am publishing a report today about the drivers of the violence in the country where you can learn a lot more about our ideas.

So thank you so much for this opportunity.

Mr. SMITH. You know, I should note that we are deeply appreciative on the subcommittee that C–SPAN has given the American people the opportunity to hear about this tragedy from experts who are living it. If you could just say how one might get that report?

Mr. AGGER. You will find it at theenoughproject.org.

Mr. SMITH. Thank you.

Ms. ROSE.

Ms. ROSE. Thank you. On the question of justice, I would have three points. So Mercy Corps, as an agency, I don't have an opinion on whether the ICC is relevant to CAR, but I will just go straight past that part of the question if that is okay.

I think there is three points to think about. One would be that we really need to be talking to Central Africans and ask them what they see as justice. That was one of the questions I asked the most when I saw—when I was on the ground. Is it community-based? Is it transitional? Is it statutory? What will make you feel safe?

And there are some funds to do those types of surveys but not enough. We certainly need more, and we need to elevate their voices in the debate. You know, Mercy Corps, Search for Common Ground, CRS, we do have some structures where we are engaging in those dialogues and putting together surveys, but it does take time.

Secondly, just to highlight that I think in the immediate term and preventing violence, community-based conciliation is the best approach. So with our GBV centers, because the justice system has ground to a halt, we have adjusted our strategy to do community-based healing and reconciliation, and we found that to have productive results.

And then just, third, I would say going back to the point about the need for state-building and support to the state, police are there, police are in Bouar, they are in Bossangoa, they are in Bambari, there are still, you know, civil servants that want to serve but they haven't been paid, so that is a peace of the justice puzzle.

And then, on the issue of gender-based violence, I do not have information on trafficking or complicity of peacekeepers, but I am happy to ask my staff and get that to you. I think regardless of whether it has happened or not, a big priority for us is ensuring that the U.N. human rights due diligence policy, which vets peacekeepers, is put into place immediately, so that any new MISCA troops that come in and those that will be transitioned up from MISCA to MINUSCA are going through that vetting process now. So the sooner the better.

And then, third, on the point of holistic services and whether we are adequately funding, Mercy Corps is funded from the Department of State, Women, Peace and Security Act/Africa Bureau for our GBV services, such as to highlight that something that started in Congress is now a funding structure and is working on the ground to really save lives.

But we aren't seeing in the international response specific carved-out funding for GBV right now. I would like to highlight that Secretary of State Kerry launched this past year, the Safe from the Start initiative that is supposed to prioritize emergency GBV response and emergency responses, so that grants would be made available. But I think CAR would be a good example to say that it is not coming to real life. We haven't seen it yet.

So thank you very much.

Mr. CAMPBELL. As far as the peacekeeping and the MISCA forces, I mean, the configuration and makeup of—from countries that border CAR is certainly a huge complication, in particular Chadian forces in there at the time.

With regard to the ICC and the ad hoc tribunals, I have nothing to share in that regard.

And then, finally, for the trafficking in CAR by the peacekeepers, I can't speculate. I have not heard of any reports myself. However, many of those countries that do border CAR have these kinds of problems, but I have to say that there have been no reports.

Thank you.

Mr. SMITH. You have all been extraordinarily insightful. Thank you for your commentary, your recommendations, as well as your relaying the facts on the ground as best you see them.

I would like to thank my colleagues for this.

Again, I want to thank C–SPAN for giving America the opportunity to hear what is going on. As Mr. Meadows said, some Americans might have a little trouble finding where CAR is on the map, but, frankly, they are our friends, our neighbors, our fellow human beings, and we need to love them, embrace them, and help them in every way possible. And so your recommendations will be very helpful, and thank you to them and for getting this message out to the rest of America.

The hearing is adjourned.

[Whereupon, at 1:43 p.m., the subcommittee was adjourned.]

APPENDIX

MATERIAL SUBMITTED FOR THE RECORD

SUBCOMMITTEE HEARING NOTICE
COMMITTEE ON FOREIGN AFFAIRS
U.S. HOUSE OF REPRESENTATIVES
WASHINGTON, DC 20515-6128

Subcommittee on Africa, Global Health, Global Human Rights, and International Organizations
Christopher H. Smith (R-NJ), Chairman

April 30, 2014

TO: MEMBERS OF THE COMMITTEE ON FOREIGN AFFAIRS

You are respectfully requested to attend an OPEN hearing of the Committee on Foreign Affairs, to be held by the Subcommittee on Africa, Global Health, Global Human Rights, and International Organizations in Room 2172 of the Rayburn House Office Building (and available live on the Committee website at www.foreignaffairs.house.gov):

DATE: Thursday, May 1, 2014

TIME: 10:00 a.m.

SUBJECT: The Central African Republic: From "Pre-genocide" to Genocide?

WITNESSES: Panel I
                    The Honorable Robert P. Jackson
                    Principal Deputy Assistant Secretary
                    Bureau of African Affairs
                    U.S. Department of State

                    The Honorable Anne Richard
                    Assistant Secretary
                    Bureau of Population, Refugees and Migration
                    U.S. Department of State

                    Panel II
                    Mr. Scott Campbell
                    Regional Director for Central Africa
                    Catholic Relief Services

                    Ms. Madeline Rose
                    Policy & Advocacy Advisor
                    Mercy Corps

                    Mr. Kasper Agger
                    Field Researcher
                    Enough Project

                    The Honorable Robin Renee Sanders
                    Chief Executive Officer
                    FEEEDS Advocacy Initiative

By Direction of the Chairman

COMMITTEE ON FOREIGN AFFAIRS

MINUTES OF SUBCOMMITTEE ON _Africa, Global Health, Global Human Rights, and International Organizations_ HEARING

Day __Thursday__ Date__ _May 1, 2014_ __Room _2172 Rayburn HOB_

Starting Time __ _10:02 a.m._ __Ending Time __ _1:43 p.m._

Recesses |__ _1_ __| (_11:14_ to _12:12_) (____to ____) (____to ____) (____to ____) (____to ____) (____to ____)

Presiding Member(s)

Rep. Chris Smith

Check all of the following that apply:

Open Session ☑   Electronically Recorded (taped) ☑
Executive (closed) Session ☐   Stenographic Record ☑
Televised ☑

TITLE OF HEARING:

The Central African Republic: From "Pre-genocide" to Genocide?

SUBCOMMITTEE MEMBERS PRESENT:

Rep. Karen Bass, Rep. Randy Weber, Rep. Tom Marino, Rep. Mark Meadows

NON-SUBCOMMITTEE MEMBERS PRESENT: _(Mark with an * if they are not members of full committee.)_

HEARING WITNESSES: Same as meeting notice attached? Yes ☑ No ☐
(If "no", please list below and include title, agency, department, or organization.)

STATEMENTS FOR THE RECORD: _(List any statements submitted for the record.)_

Revised and extended statement from Ambassador Robin Renee Sanders
Questions for the record from Rep. Chris Smith for the Department of State

TIME SCHEDULED TO RECONVENE _____
or
TIME ADJOURNED __ _1:43 p.m._

Gregory R. Simpkins
Subcommittee Staff Director

Revised and extended statement of
Ambassador Robin Renee Sanders (ret)
CEO of FEEEDS Advocacy Initiative
May 1, 2014

Mr. Chairman, Ranking Member, and Members of the Committee, I want to thank you for including me on this panel on the situation in the Central Africa Republic (CAR), and issue that I am following very closely. I have lived in and work on Central African regional issues both when I was a Director for Africa at the National Security Council and also when I was U.S. Ambassador to the Republic of Congo. The latter time was when former CAR President Bozizé first came to power; this was also a time of great conflict and human suffering in CAR. The question the Committee is seeking views on today, however, is whether or not the Central African Republic is already in the throes of a pre-genocide atmosphere or already embroiled in genocide. My remarks will address this and other elements that might be important to consider as we work together as the international community to try to stem the tide of violence and human suffering in CAR.

I first want to say something about the sheer devastation of the humanitarian crisis, having been up on the border area many times between Central Africa Republic (CAR) and Republic of Congo in years past, and in fact there remain refugees there from earlier CAR conflicts. For more than a decade instability has reigned in CAR caused by internal issues which have never been fully resolved – socially, politically, and ethnically – keeping the country environment unstable, and the people of the CAR at the mercy of the next wave of violence. Because of the continued instability and not being on the radar screen of the international community for more than a decade until the rise of the Seleka in December 2012, the events since then have set in motion two things: revenge killing by the anti-balaka Christian groups, which spawned into sectarian violence.

In addition over the last several days we are hearing unconfirmed reports of what I have been calling "reverse revenge killings" reportedly from armed Muslim militias or former Seleka running raids from Muslim enclaves in the North into nearby towns such as attacking two days ago a hospital, and killing Christians, and workers with Medicine San Frontier, near the border with Chad. These enclaves only exist because Muslims have been forced to run from sectarian violence directed at them by the anti-Balaka Christian groups. Anti-balaka groups also are preventing those Christians who want to live in peace with their Muslim neighbors from doing so.

Therefore, what we have, as you know, are the following:

- Sectarian violence;Segregated country along Christian-Muslim lines;
- Large numbers of displaced person, afraid and facing hunger
- Attacks on convoys evacuating people of either religious groups
- Looming potential for famine and further spread of disease as neither planting or harvesting season has or will take place in the violent environment
- Continued impunity of current and past leaders and perpetrators of violence and crimes against civilians, including former Seleka leader Djtodia, former president Bozize, and

anti-Balaka Christian leaders as well as Muslim leaders who are perpetrating crimes against humanity

These are elements that could possibly lead down the road to something we have not seen before: A two-way genocide as each group, Muslim and Christians, impose horrendous revenge and "reverse revenge" killing upon each other.

If we allow this to happen this will be a new challenge for the country and international community on top of the already critical humanitarian crisis with thousands of internally displaced persons (IDP's) already on the umbrella of the airport as it is the only place they feel remotely safe.

Thus, what can be suggested as the way forward? I recognize that the Administration is working full time on the humanitarian crisis with internally displaced person, but other donors also need to step up and fulfill pledges to provide assistance. The 2,000 French troops and the 5,000 African Union troops of MISCA as well as the 150 EU troops who have just arrived should all be commended, but also we need to double down on ensuring that their troops are not seen to support one religious group over another.

Having served in government for many years, I also recognize the time line needed to get the full complement of the 12,000-person UN Peace Keeping Mission in by September 2014 and that every effort is being made to advance this. But, the reality may get ahead of their arrival – and, we can see this now if we are entering a new phase of reverse revenge killings by Muslim militia. We need to consider asking the UN to also request police units from contributing countries to be added to the UN force so that areas were violence have ebbed and flowed can move from fragile stability to more permanent communities of stability.

Thus, as we balance this *triplex* of sectarian violence/revenge killings, the IDP humanitarian crisis, and looming famine we may need to jump now to concurrently work with the transition government to setup Peace Commission in rural areas; current religious enclaves; and, in Bangui because without a release valve for people to vent and articulate both their fear and hatred; stem their desire to revenge kill for atrocities done to them or their families, and address the overall environment of crimes against humanity we are likely at the beginning of seeing the current de facto segregation of CAR move into something worse - such as a two-way genocide the likes of which we have not seen before. The potential is there.

In general peace or reconciliation commissions such as in Sierra Leone, South Africa, and even the communal ones in Rwanda began in after peace – or at least fragile stability - had been restored, or in the case of South Africa when apartheid had been abolished. I am not sure we can wait for that phase in CAR. The triplex of issues we see today may prohibit reaching an end to violence and atrocities unless some release value for the hatred and disregard for humanity by the militia groups on both sides is addressed concurrently in the present environment. I recognize that many NGO groups are working to assist with workshops and reconciliation programs. But, what I am suggesting is also looking at what traditional methods of reconciliation are used in village communities and among various CAR ethnic groups, along the lines of the framework of what Rwanda used - *local traditional solution to local traditional healing.* This is the only way that sustainable peace can be maintained -- if each community can find a way to forgive each other. Of course the full healing process will take generations, but we have to start somewhere. In addition, I go back to the issue of impunity of leadership being addressed and using institutions like the International Criminal Court (ICC) to do so as a beginning. If the local population cannot see that leaders are brought to justice how can we expect them to have faith in peace and reconciliation efforts on the ground, or for those to be sustainable.

Although this is not directly part of the Committee's question today, I would be remiss if I didn't mention this issue having served as U.S. Ambassador also in Nigeria when the resurgence of Boko Haram happened. Events like we see in CAR, although we might think it cannot get worse, it can. They can spirally even more out of control so quickly, so fast. Thus, I think we need to be mindful that there is the potential for untoward groups to come into CAR and take advantage of the environment and the segregated environment of Muslims and Christians – not only fueling more hatred and violence, but also bringing with them more violent method such as terrorist tactics. I am specifically thinking of fundamentalist groups who could come in to provide Al-Qaeda-inspired terrorist training to help advance the mission of revenge and reverse revenge killings. This could happen on either side of the religious divide, not just within the Muslim segregated enclaves but also within segregated Christian segregated communities that now exist since the negative atmosphere of hatred and violent pay-back is the order of the day. We need to pay attention to this and seek to work as much as possible within these enclaves to not only distribute much-needed food, but find ways with these groups to create the space for the revenge killings to end on both sides.

Again, I want to thank the Subcommittee for allowing me to share these views, and I stand ready to answer any of your questions

**Questions Submitted to
Assistant Secretary of State Anne C. Richard by
Representative Christopher Smith
House Foreign Relations Subcommittee on Africa, Global Health,
Global Human Rights, and International Organizations
May 1, 2014**

Rep. Smith: Can you provide a list of the groups that are getting humanitarian assistance money? And, what might be anticipated going forward for faith-based organizations in this relief effort?

Ms. Richard: Please see Attachment A for a list of organizations receiving funding for humanitarian programs in CAR from the State Department and USAID. We recognize the importance of faith-based organizations in providing assistance and promoting reconciliation between religious groups in CAR. We welcome all organizations addressing humanitarian needs in CAR, including faith-based organizations, to apply for humanitarian funding through our normal funding processes. A number of our partner organizations are also working with the Interreligious Leaders Platform in CAR to amplify their voices and support their peacemaking efforts. For example, at the end of April, Catholic Relief Services, with support from USAID, organized a national campaign for social cohesion, in which Muslim, Christian, and Protestant leaders played a key role. We are also looking at ways to link the religious leaders working for peace with the media and radio programming work of our partners. USAID's Center for Faith-Based and Community Initiatives is in regular contact with faith communities in CAR and actively looking for additional ways to engage with them in peacebuilding efforts going forward. We recognize faith communities and religious leaders need to be actively engaged in preventing further violence and restoring peace in CAR.

Rep. Smith: Are other countries meeting their commitments? Could we get a list of countries – commitments made, commitments unmet? Do we have sufficient resources? (Bass also asked for a copy of this list and what Congress could do to put pressure on other countries to take on a fair share of the burden). And U.S. aid to Yemen has spread across a number of different program areas. Two questions: Is all of our aid getting marked?

Ms. Richard: The magnitude and scope of humanitarian needs in CAR continues to surpass the amount of funding available to meet those needs. While the United States has fulfilled its pledges, cash flow issues in Europe and elsewhere are contributing to a delay in the allotment of resources to the CAR response. Please see Attachment B for an outline of outstanding commitments from donor countries. The State Department and USAID are actively engaged with these donor countries through our Embassies and Missions abroad and in New York. We will continue to engage these donors on the need for their commitments to be realized now in order to meet immediate needs. Regarding the second question, all of our announced funding was specifically earmarked for the CAR response. This does not include Africa-wide contributions we have made to the Office of the U.N. High Commissioner for Refugees and the International Committee of the Red Cross which may be used for their response in CAR. Finally, there is no blanket branding and marking waiver in place for U.S. assistance in CAR, and all U.S.-funded humanitarian programs must follow normal branding and marking guidelines.

Rep. Smith: What role has the APB played? Have they met on CAR? Is the APB meeting its promise?

Ms. Richard: The situation in the CAR has been the subject of high-level U.S. interagency attention for some time, particularly since the months before the overthrow of the CAR government in early 2013. Through the APB and other standing interagency processes, the State Department and other agencies have worked to develop an effective response to the growing risk of conflict and widespread violence against civilians. The APB has been particularly helpful in elevating the CAR crisis in the attention of the interagency, identifying options for senior policy makers, and focusing U.S. efforts. The APB's focus on CAR was instrumental in quickly securing new resources for the response, particularly the $7.5 million in Complex Crises Funds (see Attachment C) and Human Rights Grants Program dedicated to peacebuilding, media support and social cohesion programming that supplemented the robust humanitarian assistance programming. The APB continues to meet regularly to ensure that the Administration is tracking emerging atrocity threats, including those in CAR; to lend policy guidance in crisis situations where helpful; and to drive the development of new capabilities to make us more effective at preventing and mitigating atrocities.

Attachment A: USG Humanitarian Funding for the CAR Crisis

Attachment B: Total Humanitarian Funding to CAR

Attachment C: Complex Crises Fund Fact Sheet

USG FY 2014 Humanitarian Funding for CAR Crisis (as of 1 May 2014)	
STATE/PRM	**$21,600,000**
International Committee of the Red Cross	$5,900,000
International Organization for Migration	$1,500,000
Office of the U.N. High Commissioner for Refugees	$13,700,000
World Food Program	$500,000
USAID/OFDA	**$16,853,349**
Action Contre le Faim (ACF)	$1,000,000
ACTED	$1,375,000
Catholic Relief Services	$650,638
Danish Refugee Council	$2,253,504
U.N. Food and Agriculture Organization	$280,623
International Medical Corps	$1,184,810
International Organization for Migration	$1,000,000
International Rescue Committee	$880,587
The Mentor Initiative	$1,500,242
U.N. Office for the Coordination of Humanitarian Affairs	$1,000,000
U.N. Department of Safety and Security	$500,000
U.N. Children's Fund	$2,727,945
World Food Program, U.N. Humanitarian Air Service	$1,000,000
World Health Organization	$1,500,000
USAID/FFP	**$28,500,000**
World Food Program	$26,000,000
UN Children's Fund	$2,500,000
TOTAL USAID AND STATE HUMANITARIAN ASSISTANCE TO CAR IN FY 2014	**$66,953,349***
*Note: Additional funding is anticipated in FY 2014.	

USG FY 2014 Conflict Mitigation, Reconciliation and Peacebuilding for CAR Crisis	
USAID/DCHA	**$7,320,000**
Catholic Relief Services	$1,820,000
Mercy Corps	$2,000,000
Search for Common Ground	$2,000,000
Internews	$1,500,000

Central African Republic		
Total Humanitarian Funding per Donor in 2014 as of 21-May-2014		
Compiled by OCHA on the basis of information provided by donors and appealing organizations. These numbers may change as donors provide additional information.		

Donor	Funding Contributed to Date (21 MAY)	Uncommitted pledges
Grand Total USD:	243,283,885	99,921,382
European Commission	26,604,961	52,016,656
Sweden	3,434,740	13,861,995
United Kingdom	8,264,464	11,730,976
Angola	0	10,000,000
World Bank	15,800,000	4,200,000
Switzerland	4,379,596	2,048,061
Luxembourg	1,437,077	2,011,199
France	8,420,215	1,638,556
African Development Bank	0	1,000,000
Italy	2,103,487	787,232
Korea, Republic of	1,460,000	300,000
Czech Republic	249,602	142,304
Ireland	3,354,765	87,851
Greece	0	68,966
Lithuania	0	27,586
United States	66,953,349	0
Central Emergency Response Fund (CERF)	19,624,767	0
Canada	14,762,004	0
Allocation of unearmarked funds by UN agencies	11,875,898	0
Denmark	8,909,330	0
Japan	6,500,000	0
Private (individuals & organisations)	5,980,722	0
Belgium	5,483,277	0
Finland	5,033,347	0
Norway	4,955,170	0
Various (details not yet provided)	4,413,809	0
Australia	3,574,620	0
Germany	3,396,345	0
Netherlands	2,779,000	0
Carry-over (donors not specified)	2,515,765	0
Austria	689,655	0
Estonia	135,686	0
Monaco	96,286	0
Slovenia	41,379	0
Malta	34,200	0
Andorra	10,345	0
Guyana	10,024	0

Complex Crises Fund: CENTRAL AFRICAN REPUBLIC

February 2014

BACKGROUND

The crisis in the Central African Republic (CAR), which had destabilized the country since late 2012, reached a critical point on December 5, 2013. Militia groups clashed in the country's capital Bangui, setting off widespread violence that has since claimed thousands of civilian lives nationwide, displaced nearly a quarter of the population, and taken on an increasingly sectarian cast. Despite efforts by community and religious leaders to quell what has already been called ethnic-religious cleansing, the conflict in CAR is at risk of sliding further into mass atrocities or genocide. Authorities have been unable to restore order and security, creating a security vacuum and exacerbating the humanitarian disaster, with an estimated half the population now in need of urgent assistance and protection. The complex crises fund was initiated in December 2013 to respond to the crisis.

PROGRAM GOAL & OBJECTIVES

USAID's Complex Crises Fund programming in CAR aims to prevent genocide and mass atrocities, expanding the space for the provision of humanitarian assistance and supporting conditions favorable to a peaceful political transition.

Objective 1: Strengthen local leaders' messaging on peace, tolerance, and non-violence. Religious and other local leaders have been vocal advocates of peace in CAR, but there is need for expanding their reach and impact. Peace messaging efforts will be crafted and led by locals, embedded into broader peace initiatives, and conducted in a way that strengthens the role of community peace leaders.

Objective 2: Strengthen local peacebuilding initiatives to foster a renewed sense of security, peaceful inter-group relations, and a foundation for rebuilding social cohesion. USAID programming will support local peace leaders to re-establish a sense of security, develop capacity to manage newly polarized relationships, and lay a foundation for rebuilding social cohesion.

Objective 3: Improve access to timely and accurate public information. Accurate, up-to-date information about the security situation and assistance activities is severely lacking in CAR, allowing rumors to flourish and sometimes leading to large-scale displacement and violent mobilization in anticipation of possible attacks. This information-action dynamic will be counteracted by expanding the availability of timely and accurate information.

ILLUSTRATIVE PROGRAM ACTIVITIES

- Work with community leaders, building their capacity to resolve inter-communal disputes peacefully
- Increase capacity of key media outlets to foster dialogue and support the transition process
- Conduct non-violence campaigns promoting tolerance in flashpoint communities
- Distribute credible information to quell rumors and promote security
- Facilitate community mapping to identify assets and vulnerabilities, leading to community-based protection and social cohesion plans

FAST FACTS:
Budget: $6 million

Start Date: February 2014 (12 months)
Partners: Mercy Corps, Search for Common Ground, Catholic Relief Services